Primary Partners®
Sharing Time

I Belong to The Church of Jesus Christ of Latter-day Saints

- 12 Learning Activities that teach the gospel

- 12 Bite-size Memorize Scripture Posters

- Preview of 66 more Learning Activities (Teaching Tools)

**"I Belong to The Church of Jesus Christ of Latter-day Saints"
Sharing Time Themes 1-12**

1. I Belong to The Church of Jesus Christ
2. I Belong to The Church of Jesus Christ of Latter-day Saints
3. I Know Who I Am
4. I Believe in the Savior, Jesus Christ
5. The Prophet Speaks for the Savior. I Can Follow the Prophet Today.
6. I Know God's Plan
7. I'll Follow Him in Faith
8. I'll Honor His Name
9. I'll Do What Is Right
10. I'll Follow His Light
11. Teachings of the Prophet
12. His Truth I Will Proclaim

D1306802

Introducing the Author and Illustrator, Creators of the Following Series of Books and CD-ROMS:

Primary Partners® manual match activities, sharing time, singing fun, and Achievement Days, *Young Women Fun-tastic! Activities for Manuals 1-3 and Personal Progress Motivators, Gospel Fun Activities, Super Singing Activities, Super Little Singers, File Folder Family Home Evenings,* and *Home-spun Fun Family Home Evenings*

Mary Ross, Author

Mary Ross is an energetic mother, and has been a Primary teacher, and Achievement Days leader. She loves to help children and young women have a good time while learning. She has studied acting, modeling, and voice. Her varied interests include writing, creating activities and children's parties, and cooking. Mary and her husband, Paul, live with their daughter, Jennifer, in Sandy, Utah.

Jennette Guymon-King, Illustrator

Jennette Guymon-King has studied graphic arts and illustration at Utah Valley College and the University of Utah. She served a mission to Japan. Jennette enjoys sports, reading, cooking, art, gardening, and freelance illustrating. Jennette and her husband Clayton, live in Riverton, Utah. They are the proud parents of their daughter Kayla Mae, and sons Levi and Carson.

Copyright © 2002 by Mary H. Ross and Jennette Guymon-King
All Rights Reserved

Covenant Communications, Inc.
American Fork, Utah

Printed in Canada
First Printing: November 2002

Primary Partners® *Sharing Time: I Belong to The Church of Jesus Christ of Latter-day Saints*
ISBN 1-59156-139-6

ACKNOWLEDGEMENTS: Thanks to Inspire Graphics (www.inspiregraphics.com) for the use of Lettering Delights computer fonts. —This product is neither sponsored nor endorsed by The Church of Jesus Christ of Latter-day Saints.

INTRODUCTION
Primary Partners
SHARING TIME
Theme: I Belong to The Church of Jesus Christ of Latter-day Saints

This volume of teaching ideas can be used year after year for Primary sharing time as well as for family home evening to teach children about belonging to the Church, and to increase their desire to live the gospel so that they can one day return to live in the presence of Heavenly Father and Jesus. Plus, using the activities for family home evening will help reinforce what children are learning in Primary.

Teaching couldn't be easier with these 12 post-and-present activities and Bite-size Memorize posters that represent the 12 "I Belong to The Church . . ." themes. Simply copy, color, laminate, and cut out the visuals and follow the instructions. If you want to give the Bite-size Memorize cards to children you can reduce and copy the posters in this book (shown right), or print the smaller forms in color or black and white from the CD-ROM.

All patterns and instructions from this book are available to print from CD-ROM (shown right) in color or black and white.

Other teaching books and CD-ROMs created for the 2003 theme "I Belong to The Church of Jesus Christ of Latter-day Saints" are described as follows and outlined on the following page. Use them for sharing time, family home evening, or classroom presentations. Each of the following books are also available on CD-ROM to print images in color or black and white.

• The *Gospel Fun Activities* book is in full color and ready-to-use. Simply tear out the perforated pages, cut out the visuals, and you have an instant sharing time or family home evening presentation.

• The *Primary Partners Teaching Tools* contains 66 activities. These are all previewed in the back of this book. Simply copy and enlarge them to present to large groups or use actual size for family home evening or individual handouts.

• The *Primary Partners Singing Fun!* contains visuals for each song, plus activities to motivate children to sing.

Singing leaders, see the page before the Table of Contents that introduces the *Super Singing Activities* and *Super Little Singers* books that are in full color and ready to use. Enjoy!

Prepare Ahead: You will need to obtain seven true stories on prayer from the Internet for Theme 7 Activity (p. 61).

2003 Themes:	Primary Partners TEACHING TOOLS book and CD-ROM (previewed on pp. 109–122)	Gospel Fun Activities all-color book and CD-ROM	Primary Partners Singing Fun! book & CD-ROM
1. I Belong to the Church of Jesus Christ	1. Six Activities on Christ Organizing His Church		1. "The Church of Jesus Christ"
2. The Church of Jesus Christ of Latter-day Saints	2. Nine Activities on the Restoration of the Church		2. "On a Golden Springtime"
3. I Know Who I Am	3. Four Activities on Being a Child of God		3. "I Am a Child of God"
4. I Believe in the Savior Jesus Christ	4. Six Activities on Believing in the Savior	4. Use Activity 9: Happy Henry and Miserable Mac Body Building Puzzles.	4. "Easter Hosanna"
5. The Prophet Speaks for the Savior. I Can Follow	5. Seven Activities on the Prophet's Teachings		5. "The Things I Do"
6. I Know God's Plan	6. Ten Activities on God's Plan of Salvation	6. Use Activities 1: Annabell's Accountable Cow Farm, 2: CTR Tools Match Game, 3: Commandment Maze, 10: Second-Coming Suitcase.	6. "I Lived in Heaven"
7. I'll Follow Him in Faith	7. Five Activities on Following Jesus Christ	7. Use Activities 4: Strong and Wilting Plant Match Game, 5: Find the Light Situation Spotlight.	7. "Lord, I Would Follow Thee"
8. I'll Honor His Name	8. Eight Activities on Honoring Jesus Christ	8. Use Activities 1, 2, and 3 (see #6 above).	8. "Choose the Right Way"
9. I'll Do What is Right	9. Six Activities on Doing What is Right	9. Use Activity 6: Trail to Holy Ghost Town Game.	
10. I'll Follow His Light	10. Eight Activities on Following His Light	10. Use Activities 4 and 5 (see #7 above), 11: My Service Garden Game to Plant Acts of Service.	
11. Teachings of the Prophet	11. Four Activities on Listening to the Prophet		
12. His Truth I Will Proclaim	12. Six Activities on Testimony & Missionaries	12. Use Activities 7: Missionary Kite Maze 8: Missionary Fish Find 12: Testimony Foundation	

Table of Contents

Primary Partners Sharing Time
"I Belong to The Church of Jesus Christ of Latter-day Saints"

THEMES 1-12:

Enjoy Full-color, Ready-to-use Presentations:

Book 1: Super Singing Activities
Book 2: Super Little Singers
to Motivate Children to Sing

With these two volumes of singing activities, there is never a dull moment in Primary and family home evening.

Use them each week along with the *Primary Partners Singing Fun!* book and CD-ROM to match the sharing time theme for the current year.

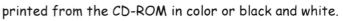

With these colored, ready-to-use visuals you can create a memorable singing experience. All of the visuals in the books can be printed from the CD-ROM in color or black and white.

Some of the activities in *Super Singing Activities* are: Melody's Family Tree, Bird in the Leafy Treetops, Build a Snowman, Christmas Tree Sing with Me, City of Enoch Singing Meter, Fill Noah's Ark Pick-a-song (shown above, right), and more.

In *Super Little Singers* you will find visuals or actions for 28 songs, plus six singing motivators.

Some of the activities in *Super Little Singers* are: I Sing Like a Bird singing motivator, action activities, visuals for seven all-time favorite children's songs, e.g., "Ants Go Matching," Eensy Weensy Spider," "Five Little Ducks," "Five Little Speckled Frogs," "Old MacDonald," "Twinkle, Twinkle, Little Star," "Wheels on the Bus," and twenty-one songs from the *Children's Songbook*.

Theme 1   I Belong to The Church of Jesus Christ

BITE-SIZE MEMORIZE

And they were in the name of were called the of.

3 Nephi 26:21

SCRIPTURE TO MEMORIZE: Memorize the 3 Nephi 26:21 Bite-size Memorize poster on page 2 (shown right). Print small posters to hand out to children from the CD-ROM.*

SONG: Sing "The Church of Jesus Christ," *Children's Songbook*, p. 77. This song is illustrated in *Primary Partners® Singing Fun!—I Belong to The Church of Jesus Christ of Latter-day Saints* book and CD-ROM.

LESSON: Ask, "Why are we baptized in the name of Jesus Christ? Why do we belong to His Church?" Answer the questions using the scriptures, Primary lessons, and sources below to teach.

• Heavenly Father loves and blesses us. He sent His Son, Jesus Christ, to earth to be our Savior (John 3:16; *Primary 1*, lesson 6; *Primary 6*, lesson 2).

• Jesus organized His Church. He ordained others to the priesthood to act in His name (Matthew 16:19; *Primary 7*, lesson 15).

• The New Testament teaches us about Christ's Church (Articles of Faith 6; *Primary 7*, lesson 9; *Gospel Principles*, chapter 16).

• When people began to change Jesus' teachings, many fell away from His Church (apostasy). The Apostles were killed, and the Lord withdrew His priesthood authority (Joseph Smith—History 1:19; D&C 1:15; *Primary 5*, lesson 2).

• See More Teaching Tools (Theme 1) previewed in the back of this book, available in the *Primary Partners® Teaching Tools— I Belong to The Church of Jesus Christ of Latter-day Saints* book or CD-ROM (to print images in color or black & white).

ACTIVITY: Jesus Christ's Church Beginning and Apostasy (Time Line Show-and-Tell)

OBJECTIVE: Help children realize that the gospel of Jesus Christ was on the earth at one time, and then taken away. Children can learn about being with Jesus and Heavenly Father in the premortal life and then following Heavenly Father's plan, which brought us to earth. Having the gospel is a great blessing.

TO MAKE VISUALS: *Copy, color, cut out, and laminate the visuals (pages 3–15), putting together the premortal life circle and earth parts A and B. Some visuals (earth, Heavenly Father, and Jesus Christ) will be used for Theme 2 presentation. The earth visual will also be used for Theme 8.

TO PRESENT: Present Theme 1 first and then Theme 2 the following month. Tell the story of Jesus organizing His Church and of the Apostasy. (Theme 2 tells of Jesus restoring His Church in the latter-days.) To present, simply read the text or say it in your own words as you post and present the visuals. Allow plenty of time for children to give their thoughts as you present the material.

*All images can be printed in full color or black and white using the CD-ROM: *Primary Partners Sharing Time—I Belong to The Church of Jesus Christ of Latter-day Saints.*

1

3 Nephi 26:21

Jesus Christ's Church Beginning and Apostasy
(Time Line Show-and-Tell)

Because Heavenly Father loves us and blesses us, He sent His Son, Jesus Christ, to the earth to be our Savior. Because Heavenly Father is our Father, the Father of all the spirits who lived in heaven, Jesus Christ is our Brother. Let's learn how much Jesus loves us and wants us to be like Him so that we can return to our Heavenly Father someday.

1 PLACE PREMORTAL WORLD, HEAVENLY FATHER, AND CHILDREN ON THE BOARD.

Before we came to this earth we lived in heaven. This was called our premortal life. Here our Heavenly Father gave us the plan of salvation.
• *Why did Heavenly Father create this wonderful plan for us?* So that we will know how to live so we can be prepared to live with Heavenly Father again someday.

2 PLACE SATAN AND 1/3 CHILDREN AND JESUS ON THE BOARD.

Satan lived in heaven with us. Jesus was also there.
Satan was wicked and did not want to obey Heavenly Father's plan.
• *What was Satan's plan for us?* Satan wanted to destroy Heavenly Father's plan of salvation.
He wanted to force us to be good and take away our free agency.
• *Did Heavenly Father accept Satan's plan?* No. Heavenly Father made Satan leave heaven. One third of the children in heaven chose not to follow Jesus. They wanted to follow Satan.
• *What happened to those children?* They were sent out of heaven with Satan. These spirits did not receive a body. They will not be able to return to live with Heavenly again someday.
TAKE SATAN AND 1/3 CHILDREN OFF BOARD.

3 Jesus lived in heaven with us. He wanted to obey Heavenly Father's plan.
• *What Did Jesus say He would do?* Jesus said He would come to earth and be our Savior. He said that we should all be free to make our own choices.
• *What did Jesus say He would do for us?* He said he would come to earth, organize His Church, and be our Savior. Heavenly Father accepted His plan.
• *What happened to those who followed Jesus?* We chose to follow Jesus and we were able to come to earth to receive a body. We were so happy that we could be created in God's image and come to earth to learn about and live Heavenly Father's plan of salvation.

4 PLACE THE EARTH ON THE BOARD.
• *Who created the earth where we now live?* Jesus was directed by Heavenly Father to create the earth. Heavenly Father's children who chose to follow Jesus are able to come and live on it.

*All images can be printed in full color or black and white using the CD-ROM:
Primary Partners Sharing Time—I Belong to The Church of Jesus Christ of Latter-day Saints.

3

5 PLACE THE PROPHETS CIRCLE ON THE BOARD.

• *How did the people learn about Heavenly Father's plan of salvation?* When we came from heaven to the earth a veil was placed over our minds and we were not able to remember our life in heaven with Heavenly Father and Jesus. So Jesus sent prophets to the earth to teach the people to be righteous. Some people obeyed and some did not.

• *Where can we read about the teachings of the prophets before Jesus came to the earth?* In the Old Testament you read about prophets such as Adam, Noah, Abraham, Moses, and others.

6 PLACE JESUS ON EARTH.

After many hundreds of years, Jesus was born on the earth. He grew up learning of Heavenly Father's plan as He prayed to Heavenly Father.

7 PLACE THE BAPTISM CIRCLE ON THE BOARD.

Jesus wanted to be baptized so He went to the River Jordan and John the Baptist baptized Him.

• *Why was Jesus baptized?* Jesus was obedient to all of Heavenly Father's commandments, so why did He need to be baptized? Jesus said that everyone mus be baptized to enter into Heavenly Father's kingdom.

8 PLACE THE HOLY GHOST CIRCLE ON THE BOARD.

When Jesus was baptized, the presence of the Holy Ghost was there.

• *When do we receive the Holy Ghost?* After we are baptized into His Church, we receive a special blessing giving us the spirit of the Holy Ghost to guide us.

9 PLACE 12 APOSTLES ON BOARD.

Jesus organized His church, calling 12 Apostles. He taught the people His gospel and how to obey Heavenly Father's commandments. He told them that as they lived Heavenly Father's plan of salvation that they would be able to return to Him someday.

10 PLACE THE COMMANDMENTS CIRCLE ON THE BOARD.

• *How did we receive the commandments of God?* The prophet Moses was given the 10 commandments by God before Jesus came to the earth. Jesus taught the people of these commandments and gave us many other commandments to follow.

11 PLACE THE MISSIONARY CIRCLE ON THE BOARD.

When Jesus called His 12 Apostles He called them His disciples. They were called "fishers of men." They were missionaries who went out and preached the gospel of Jesus Christ. They taught the people about Heavenly Father's plan of salvation.

*All images can be printed in full color or black and white using the CD-ROM:
Primary Partners Sharing Time—I Belong to The Church of Jesus Christ of Latter-day Saints.

4

12 PLACE THE SCRIPTURE CIRCLE ON THE BOARD.

Jesus taught from the scriptures. The Apostles also taught from the scriptures. Their writings about Jesus became scripture.

• *Which scriptures do we have that told about the life of Jesus while He was on the earth?*
The New Testament tells of His life on earth. Also the Book of Mormon tells of His visit to the Nephites after His death.

13 PLACE THE PRIESTHOOD CIRCLE ON THE BOARD:

Jesus gave His Apostles the priesthood, a special power.
• *What is the priesthood?* It is the power to act in God's name to perform miracles, healing and blessing the sick, performing baptisms, and performing temple ordinances.

14 PLACE THE TEMPLE CIRCLE ON THE BOARD:

Temples were built before Jesus came to the earth. As a boy He was found teaching the priests in the temple, answering their questions about Heavenly Father's plan.

15 PLACE THE SACRAMENT CIRCLE ON THE BOARD:

Before Jesus died He gave His disciples the sacrament. He told them that He was going to be crucified. He would die so that we might live again with Heavenly Father. He told them that He would be resurrected and that everyone who lives on the earth would be resurrected like Him. He blessed some bread and water and gave it to His disciples, telling them to remember His sacrifice and to always believe in Him.
• *When we partake of the sacrament each Sunday, what does the bread and water mean?* The bread represents His body, which suffered for us. The water represents His blood which He shed for us.

16 TAKE JESUS AND THE 12 APOSTLES FROM THE BOARD AS YOU SAY:

After Jesus was killed the Apostles tried to teach the Gospel and hold Jesus Christ's Church together, but many of the Apostles were also killed. After they all died, the Church could no longer stay on the earth. People began to change Jesus' teachings and many fell away resulting in the Apostasy.

17 TAKE ALL OF THE CIRCLES OFF THE BOARD AS YOU TALK ABOUT EACH.

• The SCRIPTURES, PROPHETS, and the PRIESTHOOD were taken off the earth.
• TEMPLES were no longer built or used.
• People were no longer BAPTIZED into Jesus Christ's Church as it was no longer on the earth.
• People could no longer receive the gift of the HOLY GHOST.
• MISSIONARIES were not called to preach the gospel of Jesus Christ.
• Some COMMANDMENTS were taught, but many of the correct teachings were lost.
• The SACRAMENT ordinance was taken away.
After all of these were taken away, men were left to themselves to begin their own churches.

   In another lesson (Theme 2), we will learn how The Church of Jesus Christ was restored again to the earth by the Prophet Joseph Smith (The Church of Jesus Christ of Latter-day Saints).

*All images can be printed in full color or black and white using the CD-ROM:
Primary Partners Sharing Time—I Belong to The Church of Jesus Christ of Latter-day Saints.

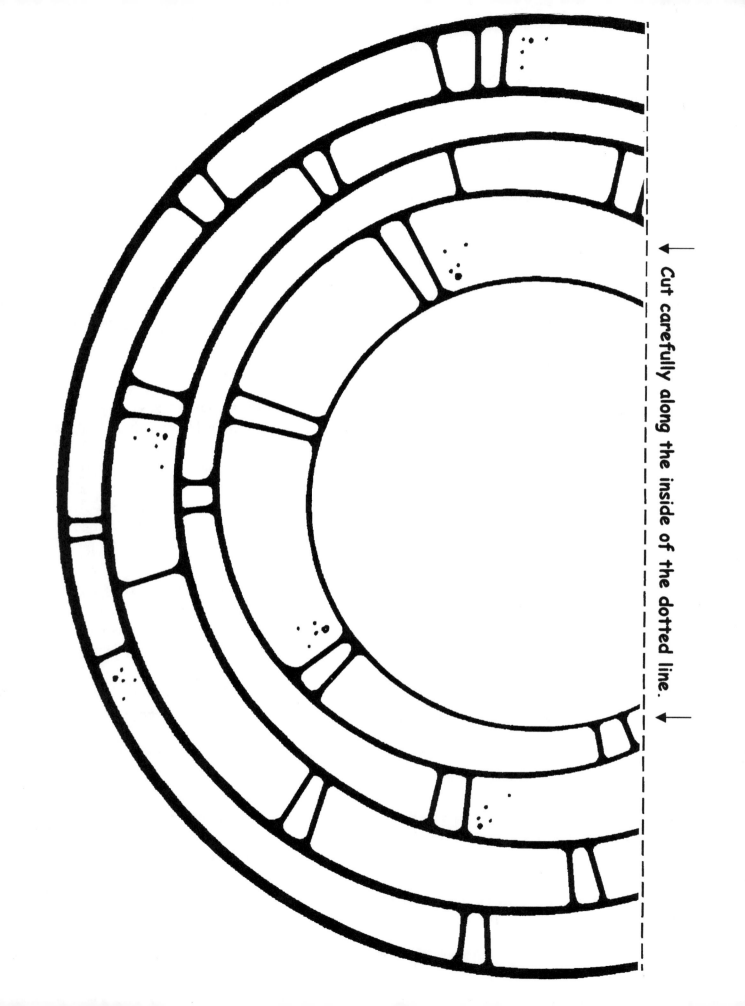

Cut carefully along the inside of the dotted line.

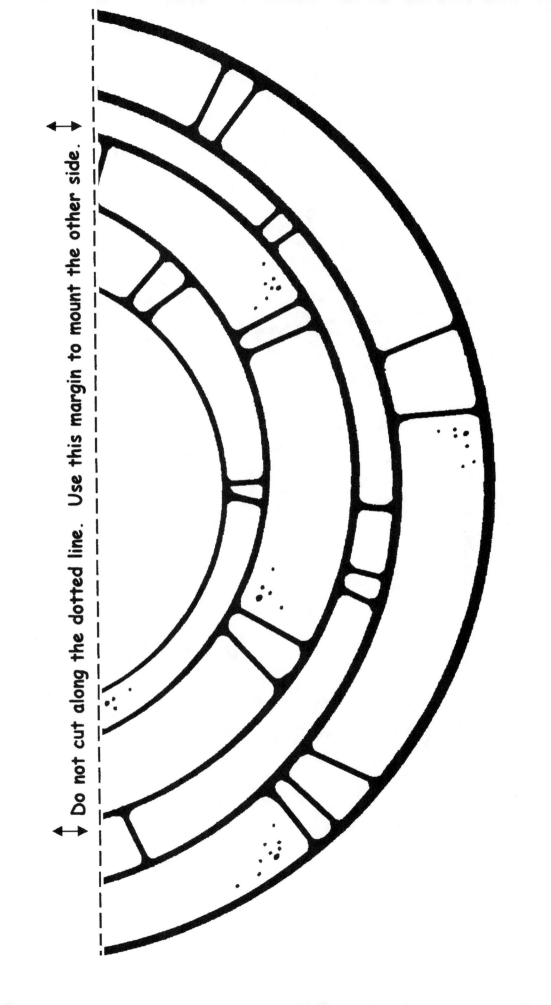

Do not cut along the dotted line. Use this margin to mount the other side.

Cut carefully along the inside of the dotted line.

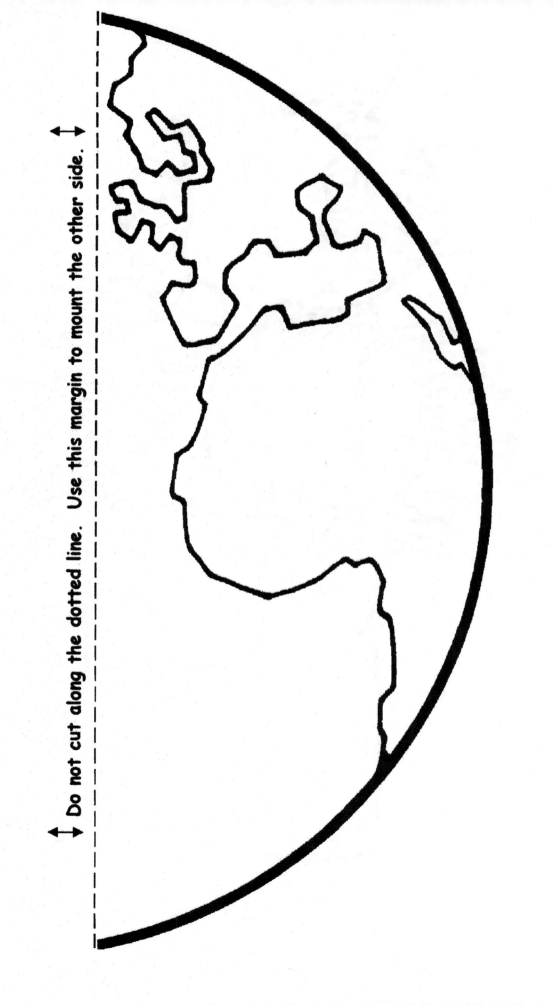

Do not cut along the dotted line. Use this margin to mount the other side.

Scriptures

Priesthood

Temples

Theme 2   I Belong to The Church of Jesus Christ of Latter-day Saints

BITE-SIZE MEMORIZE

4 thus m⁺ 👁 🏠 🐝 called in the last days, even The 🏠 of 😊 of Latter-day Saints. D&C 115:4

SCRIPTURE TO MEMORIZE: Memorize the D&C 115:4 Bite-size Memorize poster on page 17 (shown left). Print small posters to hand out to children from the CD-ROM.*

SONG: Sing "On a Golden Springtime," *Children's Songbook*, p. 88. This song is illustrated in *Primary Partners® Singing Fun!—I Belong to The Church of Jesus Christ of Latter-day Saints* book and CD-ROM.

LESSON: Ask, "What do we mean when we say we belong to The Church of Jesus Christ of Latter-day Saints?" Answer the question using the scriptures, Primary lessons, and sources below to teach.

• In the First Vision, Joseph Smith saw God the Father and His Son, Jesus Christ. He learned that Christ's true Church would be restored in these latter-days (Articles of Faith 1, 6; Joseph Smith—History 1:7-20; *Primary 5*, lesson 1).

• Joseph Smith was called to be a prophet. He translated the Book of Mormon, which contains the fulness of the gospel (Articles of Faith 8; D&C 124:125; *Primary 3*, lesson 15).

• The priesthood, ordinances, and doctrines were restored by heavenly messengers and revelation (Articles of Faith 5, 9; D&C 13:1; *Primary 5*, lessons 8, 12).

• We make and keep covenants when we become members of the Church (D&C 136:4; *Primary 3*, lesson 13; *Primary 4*, lesson 12).

• See More Teaching Tools (Theme 2) previewed in the back of this book, available in the *Primary Partners® Teaching Tools—I Belong to The Church of Jesus Christ of Latter-day Saints* book or CD-ROM (to print images in color or black & white).

ACTIVITY: Jesus Christ's Church Restored (Time Line Show-and-Tell)

OBJECTIVE: Help children learn about the period of darkness to the time the Church was restored by the Prophet Joseph Smith in the Latter-days. All of the important parts of the gospel that were taken away at the time of the Apostasy are now restored for us today. The Church of Jesus Christ (of Latter-day Saints) will remain on the earth. It will not be taken away again.

TO MAKE VISUALS: *Copy, color, cut out, and mount the visuals (pages 18-24), using the earth, Jesus and Heavenly Father from Theme 1 (pages 10-11).

TO PRESENT: Theme 2 is a continuation of Theme 1. Before presenting Theme 2, review briefly Theme 1.

To present, read the text or say it in our own words as you post and present the visuals. Allow plenty of time for children to give their thoughts as you present the material.

*All images can be printed in full color or black and white using the CD-ROM:

4 thus m⁺ called in the last days, even The of of Latter-day Saints. D&C 115:4

Jesus Christ

Jesus Christ's Church Restored (Time Line Show-and-Tell)

Heavenly Father loves us and wants us to have the blessings that come from the gospel of Jesus Christ. Many years had passed and Jesus Christ's Church was not on the earth. When it was time, the gospel was restored again. Now we can have the blessings of the gospel that were taken away after Jesus died and during the Apostasy. Heavenly Father wants us to return to Him someday so He has blessed us with the gospel in these latter-days.

1   PLACE THE EARTH, CHURCHES, AND JOSEPH SMITH ON THE BOARD:

Hundreds of years after Jesus' death and the Apostasy, the people of the world were still going through an apostasy. When Joseph Smith was a boy, he listened to the varied churches of the day telling about Jesus Christ. He wanted to join a church but was confused by the teachings of these churches. He read in James 1:5 one day, "*If any of you lack wisdom, let him ask of God, that giveth to all men liberallly, and upbraideth not; and it shall be given him.*" This meant that if he prayed, he would receive an answer as to which church he should join.

2   Joseph went to the Sacred Grove and knelt to pray to Heavenly Father. He was overtaken by an evil spirit (Satan) who tried to prevent him from praying. Joseph wanted to pray and tried harder and harder to pray. After a long time this evil power left him.

PLACE HEAVENLY FATHER AND JESUS ON THE BOARD:

Heavenly Father and Jesus appeared to Joseph. He asked them which of the churches he should join. They told him not to join any of the churches, that none of them were Jesus Christ's Church. He was later called to be the prophet of God and to organize Jesus Christ's Church upon the earth.

3   PLACE SCRIPTURES AND 12 APOSTLES ON THE BOARD:

Joseph Smith was guided by the Angel Moroni to the find the golden plates that lay hidden in the Hill Cumorah. They were an ancient record of the people called Nephites who lived on the American continent. Jesus visited these people after He died. Joseph Smith took these ancient records and translated them into the Book of Mormon. He brought scriptures to the earth. Joseph Smith has also been inspired to write other modern-day scriptures and translate other ancient records.

• *What are some of these other scriptures that we have because of the prophet Joseph Smith?* Book of Mormon, Pearl of Great Price, and Doctrine and Covenants.

The prophet Joseph called 12 Apostles just as Jesus did when He lived upon the earth to guide and direct the Church. We still have 12 Apostles today who help the prophet guide Jesus Christ's Church.

• *What is the name of Jesus Christ's Church?* The Church of Jesus Christ of Latter-day Saints.

• *Why does it say "Latter-day Saints?"* We live in the latter days where the gospel is restored and when Jesus Christ will come again.

*All images can be printed in full color or black and white using the CD-ROM:
Primary Partners Sharing Time—I Belong to The Church of Jesus Christ of Latter-day Saints.

18

4   PLACE THE OTHER CIRCLES ON THE BOARD AS YOU TALK ABOUT THEM.

When Joseph Smith organized Jesus Christ's Church on the earth again, he was instructed to bring back the blessings that were taken away.

• PROPHETS: In these latter-days, Heavenly Father and Jesus have chosen prophets to lead Jesus Christ's Church. The first Prophet was Joseph Smith, the second Brigham Young, and others followed to our current Prophet today.

• *Who is our Prophet today?* President Gordon B. Hinckley. Our Prophet receives revelation from Heavenly Father and Jesus to direct and guide Jesus' Church today.

• PRIESTHOOD: Joseph Smith and Oliver Cowdery received the priesthood from Peter, James, and John who were Apostles of Jesus Christ when He lived on the earth. We now have that same authority today to act in God's name to heal the sick, perform sacred ordinances in the temple, and do baptisms. This is a great blessing.

• *How has the priesthood blessed your life today?*

• BAPTISM: Today we can be baptized just like Jesus was when John the Baptist baptized Him in the River Jordan.

• GIFT OF THE HOLY GHOST: Today we can receive the gift of the Holy Ghost after we are baptized. We can always have this Spirit to be with us if we keep the commandments of God.

• COMMANDMENTS: Today we receive new commandments from Heavenly Father through the Prophet, the Apostles, and other General Authorities.

• TEMPLES: Today we have over 100 temples throughout the world that bless our families.

• *What blessings do the temples bring to us today?*

Families can be sealed together for eternity in the temple. Baptisms, marriages, and the sealing of parents to their children can be performed in the temple for those who have died.

• SACRAMENT: We can partake of the sacrament each week in sacrament meeting just like the Aostles partook of the sacrament when Jesus gave it to them. We can remember the sacrifice Jesus Christ made for us. He died so that we might live again and have eternal life, to live with Heavenly Father and Jesus again.

• MISSIONARIES: Today we have thousands of missionaries serving in the countries of the world. The gospel of Jesus Christ is being taught and will be taught to all the nations of the earth. The kingdom of God is going forth in these latter days to bless the earth. It will never be taken from the earth again. We can all be missionaries and share the gospel of Jesus Christ with others. Jesus said, in Moses 1:39: "This is my work and my glory—to bring to pass the immortality and eternal life of man."

We are truly blessed to have the gospel today.

IF THERE IS TIME, ASK A FEW CHILDREN BEAR THEIR TESTIMONY.

Theme 3   I Know Who I Am

BITE-SIZE MEMORIZE

All of U
R 👧👦
of the
most High.

Psalm 82:6

SCRIPTURE TO MEMORIZE: Memorize the Psalm 82:6 Bite-size Memorize poster on page 26 (shown right). Print small posters to hand out to children from the CD-ROM.*

SONG: Sing "I Am a Child of God," *Children's Songbook*, p. 2. This song is illustrated in *Primary Partners® Singing Fun! I Belong to The Church of Jesus Christ of Latter-day Saints.*

LESSON: Ask, "Do you know who you are and where you came from?" Answer the questions using the scriptures, Primary lessons, and sources below to teach.

• I am a child of God and lived in heaven before I came to earth (D&C 93:29; 76:24; *Primary 2,* lesson 3).

• I am a child of God blessed with divine nature (3 Nephi 27:27; *The Family: A Proclamation to the World*, paragraphs 1-2; *Primary 1*, lesson 1).

• I am a child of God. He has given me spiritual gifts and talents (Articles of Faith 7; D&C 46:11; *Primary 5*, lesson 19).

• I am a child of God. I will serve my family and others (Mosiah 2:17; *Primary 2*, lesson 39; *Primary 6*, lesson 10, enrichment activities).

• See More Teaching Tools (Theme 3) previewed in the back of this book, available in the *Primary Partners® Teaching Tools—I Belong to The Church of Jesus Christ of Latter-day Saints* book or CD-ROM (to print images in color or black & white).

ACTIVITY: I Know Who I Am
(Because I Am a Child of God Match Game)

OBJECTIVE: Help children realize how special they are, that they are children of God who has a purpose for their life. The gospel of Jesus Christ gives them that purpose.

TO MAKE VISUALS: *Copy, color, cut out, and laminate the visuals (pages 27-32).

To Make the Cards: Cut each set of cards in half where indicated. Write on the back of each small half-card a number 1-12 randomly so each card has a different number. Write on the back of each large half-card a letter A-L randomly. This will help children identify the cards when they try to match them choosing a number and a letter, e.g., 6 and A.

TO PRESENT: Ahead of time, tape the cards facedown on the board, placing the small half-cards on the far left and the large half-cards on the far right. Introduce activity by saying, "We are all children of God. We know that Heavenly Father loves us and has a plan for us to return to Him. We can do many things to show Heavenly Father our love. Let's play a match game to see how special we are." Have children take turns turning over a number card (from the left) and a letter card (from the right) to make a match. When a match is made, mount the matched set on the center of the board. Have children read the card aloud and then talk about what it means.

All of U R
of the
most High.

Psalm 82:6

Because I am
a child of God...

...I can learn a
language and teach the
gospel in other lands.

Because I am
a child of God...

...I can develop talents
in music to uplift and
inspire goodness.

Because I am
a child of God...

...I can love and care
for those around me.

Because I am
a child of God...

...I can attain great
knowledge as I study,
pray, and ask Heavenly
Father for His blessing.

Because I am a child of God...

...I have a body created in Heavenly Father's image.

Because I am a child of God...

...I came from Heavenly Father's presence where I was loved and taught.

Because I am a child of God...

...Heavenly Father has a special plan for my life.

Because I am a child of God...

...I can return to Heavenly Father's presence if I follow His commandments.

Because I am
a child of God...

...I can be an example
for others as I
follow Jesus Christ.

Because I am
a child of God...

I love you!

...I can comfort others
with my love and
tender words.

Because I am
a child of God...

...I can know truth
as the Holy Ghost
touches my heart and
speaks to my mind.

Because I am
a child of God...

...I can receive
revelation for my
life as Heavenly
Father guides me.

Theme 4   I Believe in the Savior, Jesus Christ

SCRIPTURE TO MEMORIZE: Memorize the Matthew 16:16 Bite-size Memorize poster on page 34 (shown right). Print small posters to hand out to children from the CD-ROM.*

SONG: Sing "Easter Hosanna," *Children's Songbook*, p. 68. This song is illustrated in *Primary Partners® Singing Fun!—I Belong to The Church of Jesus Christ of Latter-day Saints* book and CD-ROM.

LESSON: Ask, "Do you know who the Savior Jesus Christ is and have faith in Him?" Answer the questions using the scriptures, Primary lessons, and sources below to teach.

- Jesus is the Savior of all mankind. I have faith in the Lord Jesus Christ (Articles of Faith 4; Mosiah 3:9; *Primary 4*, lesson 43).
- As I have faith, I want to repent and be baptized (Mosiah 18:10; *Primary 2*, lesson 12; *Primary 4*, lesson 14).
- I will receive the gift of the Holy Ghost (2 Nephi 32:5; *Primary 1*, lesson 7; *Primary 2*, lesson 13).
- As I choose the right each day, I can return to Heavenly Father (D&C 6:13; *Primary 2*, lesson 14; *Primary 3*, lesson 3).
- See More Teaching Tools (Theme 4) previewed in the back of this book, available in the *Primary Partners® Teaching Tools—I Belong to The Church of Jesus Christ of Latter-day Saints* book or CD-ROM (to print images in color or black & white).

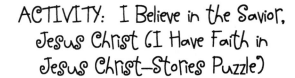

ACTIVITY: I Believe in the Savior, Jesus Christ (I Have Faith in Jesus Christ—Stories Puzzle)

OBJECTIVE: Help children learn the stories of Jesus so that they will know that He is the Savior.

TO MAKE VISUALS: *Copy, color, cut out, and laminate the Jesus picture and puzzle pieces (pages 35-41). Before laminating puzzle pieces, cut out and glue the stories on the backs.

TO PRESENT:

1. Ahead of time mount the picture of Jesus on the board and the puzzle pieces randomly to the far left and right of the board.

2. Tell children, "You can learn to believe in the Savior Jesus Christ and to increase your faith in Him as we read the stories of Jesus." Have children come up one at a time and choose a puzzle piece and read the story of Jesus on the back.

3. Have children post the puzzle piece on the poster, matching the stars to put the puzzle into place.

*All images can be printed in full color or black and white using the CD-ROM:
Primary Partners Sharing Time—I Belong to The Church of Jesus Christ of Latter-day Saints.

33

Thou art the [Christ], the [☀] of the living God.

Matthew 16:16

Because I believe in Jesus Christ,

Cut carefully along the inside of the dotted line.

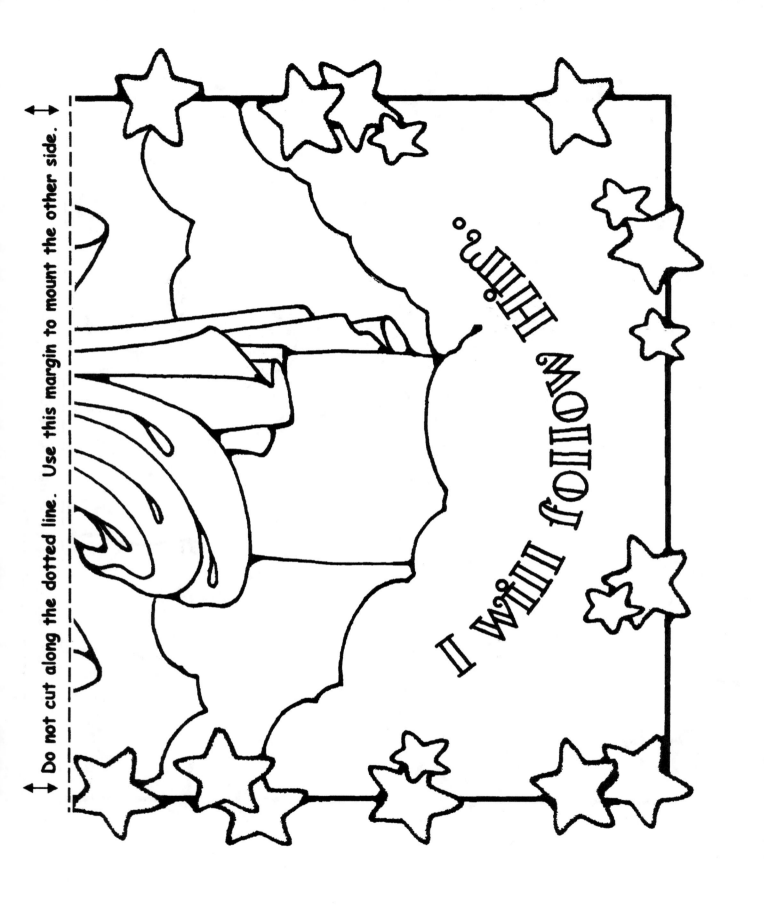

I will follow Him.

JESUS LEARNED THE GOSPEL AS A BOY: When Jesus was a boy he learned many things by reading the scriptures and praying to Heavenly Father. At age 12 He went with Joseph and Mary into Jerusalem. When it was time to return home Mary and Joseph left, thinking Jesus was with His friends. When they found that he was not, they were worried and went back to Jerusalem. They found Him in the temple talking to the wise teachers. To their surprise Jesus knew the answers to their important gospel questions. He told His parents that He was there doing His Father's work. Jesus was working to help Heavenly Father by teaching the gospel and being a missionary. (Luke 2) I WILL FOLLOW JESUS AND TEACH THE GOSPEL TO OTHERS.

JESUS PREPARED FOR HIS MISSION: Jesus went into the wilderness to be with God and to prepare for His mission. He stayed there 40 days. He fasted, going without eating or drinking anything. After 40 days Satan tried to tempt Jesus three times. He wanted Him to turn stones into bread, but He would not, even though He was hungry. Satan told him he could have all the kingdoms and money if He would do as he said. After listening to the temptations, Jesus said "no" and told Satan to go away. (Matthew 4) I CAN RESIST TEMPTATION LIKE JESUS.

JESUS TAUGHT OTHERS TO PRAY: Jesus taught His disciples (Apostles) and others how to pray. Jesus told the people they should not pray in the streets where others could see them. They should pray where they could be alone. He said some people pray, saying the same words over and over and that we should think about what we say. We should begin our prayers by saying "Our Father . . . in Heaven," thank Heavenly Father, and then ask Heavenly Father for help. Then say "Amen." Then Heavenly Father will answer our prayers and bless us. I CAN PRAY TO HEAVENLY FATHER LIKE JESUS.

JESUS WAS BAPTIZED: John the Baptist lived in the desert for many years teaching about Jesus Christ who would come and start His church. He told the people to repent of their sins and be baptized. He said Jesus would give the Holy Ghost to them when He came. He told the people Jesus was the Savior. Jesus came to John one day while he was baptizing people in the Jordan River. Jesus asked John to baptize Him. John said Jesus did not need to be baptized because He was righteous and did not sin. Jesus told John to baptize Him, that God commanded all people to be baptized. Jesus was then baptized so He could obey all of God's commandments. When Jesus came out of the water the Holy Ghost came to Him, then God spoke from heaven saying, "This is my beloved Son." (Matthew 3, Luke 3, Matthew 3, 2 Nephi 31) I CAN BE BAPTIZED LIKE JESUS.

JESUS LOVED THE LITTLE CHILDREN: When Jesus was with His disciples, some people asked Jesus to bless their children. The disciples knew Jesus was very tired and asked the people not to bring their children to Him. Jesus loved the little children and wanted to see them. He asked His disciples to bring the children to Him. Then He blessed the children and let them know He loved them. The children loved Jesus very much. Jesus told His disciples that we should have faith like little children and then we could live with God in heaven. (Mark 10:13-15) I WILL BE KIND AND LOVE OTHERS LIKE JESUS.

JESUS USED HIS PRIESTHOOD: One day Jesus and His disciples (Apostles) were on a boat on the Sea of Galilee. Jesus fell asleep and the wind began to blow high waves on the boat, filling it with water. The disciples were afraid the boat would sink, so they awoke Jesus, asking Him for help. Jesus stood, commanded the wind to stop blowing, and told the waves to go down. Jesus asked the Apostles why they were afraid and told them they should have more faith. **I WILL HAVE FAITH LIKE JESUS.**

JESUS RAISED LAZARUS FROM THE DEAD: A man named Lazarus lived in Bethany with his sisters Mary and Martha. They all loved Jesus very much. One day while Jesus was away teaching in another town, Lazarus became sick. Jesus was asked to go and heal him. By the time He got there, Lazarus had been dead four days. Jesus asked Martha to believe in Him, that Lazarus would live again. Martha told Jesus that she believed. She knew Jesus was the Savior. Mary and many others followed Jesus, crying. At the cave where Lazarus was buried Jesus asked them to remove the stone. Jesus prayed to Heavenly Father and then spoke in a loud voice telling Lazarus to come out of the cave. Lazarus came out alive! The people saw the miracle and knew Jesus was the Savior. (John 11) **I WILL HAVE FAITH IN THE PRIESTHOOD POWER WHICH HELPED JESUS HEAL OTHERS.**

JESUS SUFFERS IN THE GARDEN: Jesus and some of His Apostles went to the Garden of Gethsemane. Jesus left them to pray, knowing that He would soon need to suffer for the sins of all people who would repent. Jesus didn't want to suffer, but He wanted to obey Heavenly Father and show His great love for us. Someone needed to pay the price for our sins. Jesus was suffering great pain when an angel came to Him to strengthen Him so He could complete what He needed to do. He was sad for all the sins of the world. His whole body shook and hurt as He bled and suffered for the sins of all men.
I WILL REPENT OF MY SINS AND FOLLOW JESUS.

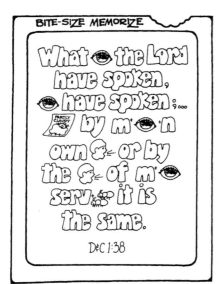

BITE-SIZE MEMORIZE

What the Lord have spoken, have spoken;... by mine own eye or by the eye of my serve it is the same.

D&C 1:38

Theme 5   The Prophet Speaks for the Savior. I Can Follow the Prophet Today

SCRIPTURE TO MEMORIZE: Memorize the D&C 1:38 Bite-size Memorize poster on page 43 (shown left). Print small posters to hand out to children from the CD-ROM.*

SONG: Sing "The Things I Do," *Children's Songbook,* p. 170. This song is illustrated in *Primary Partners® Singing Fun!—I Belong to The Church of Jesus Christ of Latter-day Saints* book and CD-ROM.

LESSON: Ask, "How can the prophet (President of the Church) today speak for the Savior? How can we follow the prophet's teachings today? What are some things the Prophet has said that we can share with our family?" Answer the questions using the scriptures, Primary lessons, and sources below.

• A prophet is a man called by our Father in Heaven to speak for Him (Exodus 3:1-6, 9-12; 1 Samuel 3:1-10, 19-20; Moses 6:26-39; Joseph Smith—History 1:11-20; *Primary 1*, lesson 43; *Gospel Principles*, chapter 9).

• The living Prophet is a special witness of Jesus Christ. He bears testimony of Heavenly Father and Jesus Christ (D&C 27:12; 1 Nephi 10:5; Jacob 7:11).

• The testimony of the Prophet strengthens my faith in Jesus Christ and guides us in these latter days (Jacob 4:4-5; D&C 76:19-23; examples from conference talks in the *Friend, Ensign,* and *Liahona*).

• See More Teaching Tools (Theme 5) previewed in the back of this book, available in the *Primary Partners® Teaching Tools—I Belong to The Church of Jesus Christ of Latter-day Saints* book or CD-ROM (to print images in color or black & white).

ACTIVITY: The Prophets Who Spoke for the Savior (Post a Prophet Clue Game)

OBJECTIVE: Help children learn of prophets who spoke for the Savior, who testified of Him.

TO MAKE VISUALS: *Copy, color, cut out, and laminate the Prophets (pp. 44-51), and cut out the clue cards (pp. 51-53).

TO PRESENT: Tell children, "Let's see how many prophets you know by playing this *Post a Prophet Clue* game. What do you know about the prophets? Can you guess who they are by listening to the clues? Let's see just how much you know."

To Play:

1. Divide children into teams, or play by having children raise their hands when they know the answer.

2. The leader pulls out a cue card and reads the first clue, then the second, and then the third, giving the children 30 seconds to guess between each clue. Tell children they are not allowed to shout out the answer.

3. If playing in teams, and the team doesn't guess the prophet, give the other team a chance to guess, reading the clues again. If they can't guess with these clues, the leader can give more obvious clues they might know.

4. When the prophet is guessed, give that child the prophet picture to post on the board or wall.

*All images can be printed in full color or black and white using the CD-ROM:
Primary Partners Sharing Time—I Belong to The Church of Jesus Christ of Latter-day Saints.

42

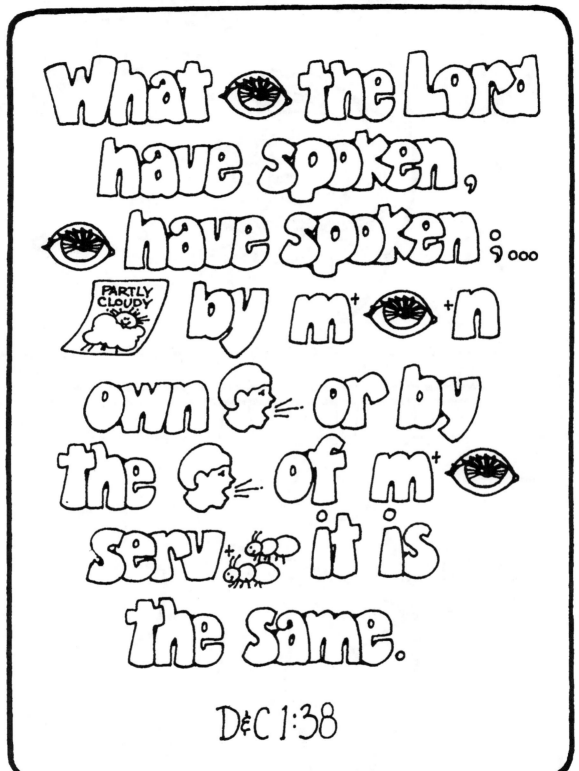

What [eye] the Lord have spoken, [eye] have spoken;... by m[+][eye][+]n own [mouth] or by the [mouth] of m[+] [eye] serv[ants] it is the same.

D&C 1:38

Enoch

Gordon B.
Hinckley

Alma

Brigham Young

Nephi

Moses

Daniel

Abinadi

Abraham

Noah

Jonah

King Benjamin

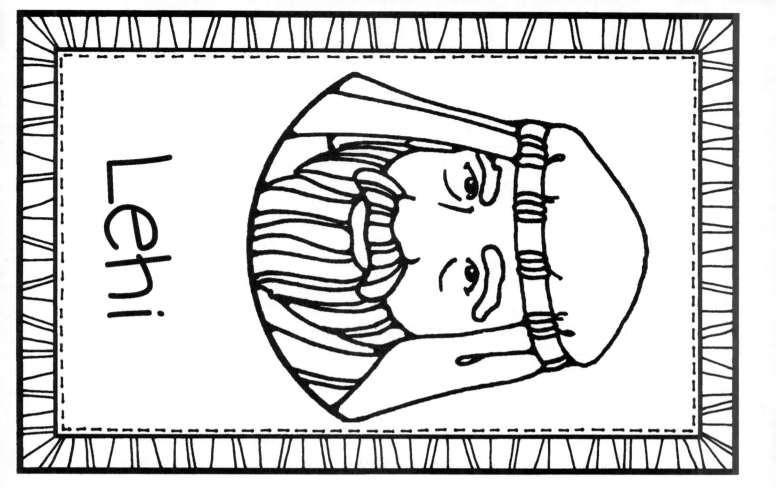

Lehi

Clue 1: This Hebrew prophet testified of Christ 1100 years before Christ's birth.

Clue 2: This prophet became a judge in Israel, restoring law and order and righteous worship in the land.

Clue 3: After Saul became their first king, This prophet gave up the judgement seat because he wanted to continue being a prophet to teach the people about Christ and to repent.

Samuel

Clue 3: This prophet taught of Jesus Christ's resurrection and prophecied that the Book of Mormon would come forth.
Clue 2: This prophet wanted to know about his father's vision of the Tree of Life.
Clue 3: This prophet was to go on a dangerous mission to retrieve a sacred record. He knew the Lord would prepare a way for him to do it.

Nephi

Clue 1: This prophet's wife was named Sarah.
Clue 2: This prophet was promised that his seed (children) would be numbered as the sand in the sea shore.
Clue 3: This prophet was commanded to sacrifice his only son Isaac. Just when he was about to let his son die, an angel told him not to. God was happy he obeyed him.

Abraham

Clue 1: This prophet lived in Jerusalem 600 years before the birth of Jesus.
Clue 2: This prophet prayed that the wicked people in Jerusalem would repent or they would be destroyed. He told them of Jesus Christ.
Clue 3: This prophet had a vision of the tree of life.

Lehi

Clue 1: This Israelite prophet grew up in the Pharaoh 's house thinking he was an Egyptian.
Clue 2: This prophet brought plagues upon Egypt so the Pharaoh would free the Israelites. When they were free, he led them to the promised land.
Clue 3: This prophet spoke with God and received the 10 Commandments.

Moses

Clue 1: This prophet told the wicked people to repent or they would be destroyed. The people did not repent.
Clue 2: This Old Testament prophet trusted in God, who told him how to save his people.
Clue 3: This prophet was commanded to take his family and two of each animal into the ark to be saved from the flood.

Noah

Clue 1: God told this prophet to go to Nineveh to warn the people to repent.
Clue 2: This prophet went to sea instead of doing as God commanded and he was swallowed by a whale.
Clue 3: This prophet repented and the fish put him on dry land. He went to Nineveh and told the people to repent. Because they repented they were not destroyed.

Jonah

Clue 1: This prophet was the head servant of the king.
Clue 2: This prophet won the favor of King Nebuchadnezzar by his power of interpreting dreams.
Clue 3: This prophet was thrown into a den of lions because he continued to pray in spite of a new law that outlawed prayer. God shut the lions' mouths.

Daniel

Clue 1: This prophet prayed to know which church was true and saw Heavenly Father and Jesus Christ.
Clue 2: The Angel Moroni visited this prophet in a vision.
Clue 3: This prophet translated the Book of Mormon.

Joseph Smith

Clue 1: Before this prophet became a prophet he became discouraged on his mission and his father wrote to him saying, "forget about yourself and go to work," and he did. Clue 2: This prophet has traveled to more countries than any other prophet to preach the gospel. Clue 3: This prophet has dedicated seventy-seven temples of the 100 plus temples that were built in his lifetime. Gordon B. Hinckley	Clue 1: This Nephite prophet was the only one who accepted the teachings of the prophet Abinadi. Clue 2: This prophet taught the people the words of the prophet Abinadi. Clue 3: This prophet led many to believe in Jesus Christ, baptizing them in the Waters of Mormon. Alma
Clue 1: This prophet lived during a time when most of the people on the earth were wicked and did not believe in God. Clue 2: This prophet taught the people to repent and obey God's commandments, and if they were righteous they could live in heaven again. Clue 3: This prophet is the one who helped the righteous people build a beautiful city called Zion. God took the whole city to heaven. Enoch	Clue 1: This prophet told the people that unless they repented and turned to Jesus Christ, they would be brought to bondage (slavery) and no one would deliver them except the Lord. Clue 2: This prophet testified of Christ to a wicked King and his followers. He was protected until he could say what the Lord wanted him to say. Clue 3: This prophet was told to take back his testimony of Jesus or be killed. He would not change his words and suffered death by fire. Abinadi
Clue 1: After this prophet arrived in the Salt Lake valley he directed the people to build a temple, plant crops, and start a new life. Clue 2: This prophet led the pioneers to Utah after they were driven out of their homes in Kirtland, Ohio; Jackson County, Missouri; and Nauvoo, Illinois. Clue 3: When this prophet arrived in Salt Lake he looked at the valley below and said, "This is the place." Brigham Young	Clue 1: This prophet was a righteous Nephite. Clue 2: This prophet taught the people that the way to serve God is to serve each other. Clue 3: Even though this prophet was a king, he did not ask the people to work to support him; he labored with his own hands so that he might serve the people. King Benjamin

Theme 6   I Know God's Plan

SCRIPTURE TO MEMORIZE: Memorize the Moses 1:39 Bite-size Memorize poster on page 55 (shown left). Print small posters to hand out to children from the CD-ROM.*

SONG: Sing "The Things I Do," *Children's Songbook,* p. 170. This song is illustrated in *Primary Partners® Singing Fun!—I Belong to The Church of Jesus Christ of Latter-day Saints* book and CD-ROM.

LESSON: Ask, "What is Heavenly Father's plan for us?" Answer the questions using the scriptures, Primary lessons, and sources below to teach.

• Jesus is my Savior. Because of Him I can have eternal life (Articles of Faith 3; *Primary 4,* lesson 45; *Primary 6,* lesson 45).

• Heavenly Father and Jesus created the earth and all forms of life. I can treat the earth and all living things with respect (3 Nephi 9:15; *Primary 6,* lessons 1, 3).

• Agency is a gift from Heavenly Father. As I choose between right and wrong, I am accountable (Articles of Faith 2; Alma 34:32; *Primary 2,* lesson 5).

• I have been sent to a family to learn to follow Jesus (1 Nephi 1:1; *Primary 2,* lesson 6; *Primary 3,* lesson 28).

• See More Teaching Tools (Theme 6) previewed in the back of this book, available in the *Primary Partners® Teaching Tools—I Belong to The Church of Jesus Christ of Latter-day Saints* book or CD-ROM (to print images in color or black & white).

ACTIVITY: I Know God's Plan (Consequences Countenance Game)

OBJECTIVE: Help children realize that each choice they make has a consequence that affects the way we feel. Our feelings show on our face, changing our countenance.

TO MAKE VISUALS: *Copy, color, and cut out parts A and B of the *Consequence Countenance* game board, arrow, and cards (pages 56–60). Glue the board parts A and B together where indicated and laminate the entire board. Then laminate the arrow and cards. Place the arrow in the center with a paper fastener (metal brad). Place the cards in a container.

TO PRESENT: Tell children that each choice they make has a consequence. Something happens because you made that decision. If good choices are made, there will be good consequences (good things will happen) and your countenance (facial expression) will show that you are happy, strong, calm, or peaceful (point to the game board). If bad choices are made, there will be bad consequences (bad things will happen) and your countenance will show that you are angry, weak, or sad.

To Play the Consequence Countenance Game: Divide children into two teams. Have one team at a time draw a decision card and hand it to the leader to read. The leader reads the situation but not the A or B choices. Ask a team player to guess which choice is the right choice without knowing what the choices are. Have them choose A or B and then read the decision they made (A or B). Choose a child from their team to come up and move the arrow to the countenance on the Consequence Countenance board that matches their choice, e.g., "peace." Award a point if the choice was right. No points are awarded if the choice was a wrong choice. Then read the other choice and turn the arrow to the Consequence Countenance, e.g., "guilty." Discuss how the different choices affect them. The team with the most points (or brightest countenance) wins!

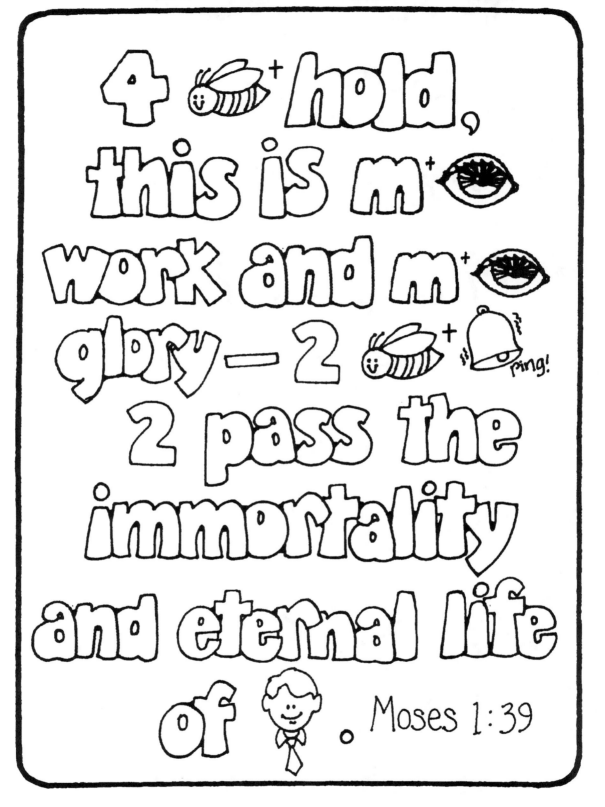

4 🐝† hold, this is m†👁 work and m†👁 glory — 2 🐝†🔔 ping! 2 pass the immortality and eternal life of 👦. Moses 1:39

CONSEQUENCE

Weak

Sad

Peace

Calm

Cut carefully along the inside of the dotted line.

COUNTENANCE

Angry

Guilty

Happy

Strong

↕ Do not cut along the dotted line. Use this margin to mount the other side. ↕

HONESTY:

Johnny saw a baseball card that he had always wanted in the store. He didn't have the money to pay for it and the store clerk was busy with another customer. What did Johnny do?

A. Johnny stole the baseball card. Every time he looked at it on the way home he felt <u>guilty</u> because he knew it was wrong to steal.

B. Johnny decided to do some extra work for his Dad to pay for the card, if it was still there. He felt <u>peace</u> knowing he didn't take what wasn't his.

KINDNESS:

Laura wanted so much to be popular at school. She wanted to be friends with a group of girls who seemed to have the most friends. Even though she didn't know these girls very well, what did Laura do?

A. She went up to the girls and started talking to them. They seemed to like her and asked her to go with them after school to play a trick on their teacher. After she did, Laura felt <u>sad</u>, wishing she had chosen better friends.

B. She asked the girls if she could hang out with them. They said she could if she didn't bring her friend Cindy. Laura said "no" because Cindy was her good friend. She felt <u>happy</u> that she was kind and true to her friendship with Cindy.

SWEARING:

Maddy was careful not to use bad words around her friends, but this new friend kept saying the same bad word over and over again. What did Maddy do?

A. Maddy asked her friend to not say that word anymore. She explained that she was taught that the word was bad. Her friend said she would try not to say it and Maddy went home feeling <u>calm</u> about saying something.

B. Maddy was so caught up in copying her friend that she started saying the bad word she heard so often. When her parents heard her say it they were angry with her and Maddy started feeling <u>angry</u> she had said it.

WORD OF WISDOM:

Kevin's new friends wanted him to go with them. They were going to smoke a cigarette for the first time. Even though he knew it was unhealthy, what did Kevin do?

A. Kevin knew that keeping the Word of Wisdom would make him feel <u>strong</u>. He knew that it was important to take care of his body, and it was also important to do what is right. He said "no."

B. Kevin decided to try smoking just one cigarette. It made him cough. When he got home he felt weak physically, but he also felt <u>weak</u> because he didn't have the courage to say "no" when he really knew it was wrong.

JEALOUSY:

Erika was the Brians' favorite babysitter. Sometimes her friend Mindy went with her to babysit. Mindy started calling the Brians and asking if she could babysit. When Erika found out, what did she do?

A. Erika felt <u>angry</u> that Mindy would try to take her job away from her so she stopped calling Mindy and pretended that she wasn't at home when Mindy would call.

B. Erika thought about Mindy, knowing she didn't get asked to babysit very often. She decided to be happy that Mindy was asked to babysit. Because she decided to share, she felt <u>calm</u> about their friendship.

FORGIVENESS:

Jessy liked to ride horses on his friend Jed's farm. The last few times he tried to ride, Jed would spook his horse so his horse would buck him off. What did Jessy do?

A. Jessy asked his friend Nick what he could do to pay Jed back by spooking his horse. Jessy tried this and Jed got hurt. Jessy felt <u>sad</u> that he tried to get even.

B. Jessy asked Jed why he tried to spook his horse and that he didn't like it. Jed said he thought it would be fun, and he was sorry he did it. Jessy was <u>happy</u> that he talked to Jed and forgave him.

SABBATH DAY:

Amy's friend Sarah asked her to stay the weekend. When she arrived, they said they were going boating on Sunday. What did Amy do?

A. Amy thought about what her parents would say about breaking the Sabbath, so she told Sarah that her mother would come and get her since she wanted to go to Church on Sunday. After Church she felt <u>peace</u>.

B. Amy told Sarah that she'd never been boating and it would be fun! After they went she felt <u>guilty</u> for going because she knew that it was not keeping the Sabbath day holy.

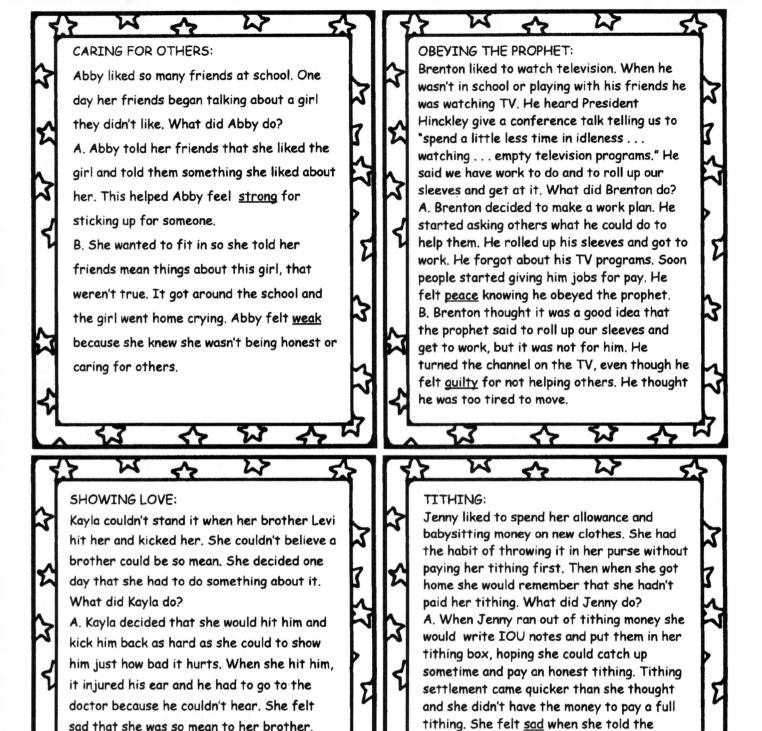

CARING FOR OTHERS:

Abby liked so many friends at school. One day her friends began talking about a girl they didn't like. What did Abby do?

A. Abby told her friends that she liked the girl and told them something she liked about her. This helped Abby feel <u>strong</u> for sticking up for someone.

B. She wanted to fit in so she told her friends mean things about this girl, that weren't true. It got around the school and the girl went home crying. Abby felt <u>weak</u> because she knew she wasn't being honest or caring for others.

OBEYING THE PROPHET:

Brenton liked to watch television. When he wasn't in school or playing with his friends he was watching TV. He heard President Hinckley give a conference talk telling us to "spend a little less time in idleness . . . watching . . . empty television programs." He said we have work to do and to roll up our sleeves and get at it. What did Brenton do?

A. Brenton decided to make a work plan. He started asking others what he could do to help them. He rolled up his sleeves and got to work. He forgot about his TV programs. Soon people started giving him jobs for pay. He felt <u>peace</u> knowing he obeyed the prophet.

B. Brenton thought it was a good idea that the prophet said to roll up our sleeves and get to work, but it was not for him. He turned the channel on the TV, even though he felt <u>guilty</u> for not helping others. He thought he was too tired to move.

SHOWING LOVE:

Kayla couldn't stand it when her brother Levi hit her and kicked her. She couldn't believe a brother could be so mean. She decided one day that she had to do something about it. What did Kayla do?

A. Kayla decided that she would hit him and kick him back as hard as she could to show him just how bad it hurts. When she hit him, it injured his ear and he had to go to the doctor because he couldn't hear. She felt <u>sad</u> that she was so mean to her brother.

B. She decided to tell her brother that she loved him and that she wanted to be his friend. She asked him not to hit or kick her anymore. Her brother was surprised that she would say she wanted to be his friend. This made Kayla feel <u>happy</u>.

TITHING:

Jenny liked to spend her allowance and babysitting money on new clothes. She had the habit of throwing it in her purse without paying her tithing first. Then when she got home she would remember that she hadn't paid her tithing. What did Jenny do?

A. When Jenny ran out of tithing money she would write IOU notes and put them in her tithing box, hoping she could catch up sometime and pay an honest tithing. Tithing settlement came quicker than she thought and she didn't have the money to pay a full tithing. She felt <u>sad</u> when she told the bishop "no," it wasn't a full tithe.

B. Jenny took one of her outfits back to the store and got the money back so she had enough to pay her tithing. She felt <u>happy</u> that she paid her tithing because shew knew that Heavenly Father would bless her for being obedient.

Theme 7   I'll Follow Him in Faith

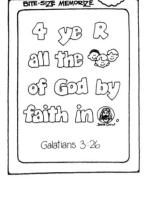

BITE-SIZE MEMORIZE

4 ye R all the 👁👁 of God by faith in 😊.

Galatians 3:26

SCRIPTURE TO MEMORIZE: Memorize the Galatians 3:26 Bite-size Memorize poster on page 62 (shown right). Print small posters to hand out to children from the CD-ROM.*

SONG: Sing "Lord, I Would Follow Thee," *Children's Songbook*, p. 220. This song is illustrated in *Primary Partners® Singing Fun!—I Belong to The Church of Jesus Christ of Latter-day Saints* book and CD-ROM.

LESSON: Ask, "How can we follow Jesus in Faith?" Answer the questions using the scriptures, Primary lessons, and sources below to teach.

• I can pray to Heavenly Father anytime, anywhere (Alma 34:19-27; *Primary 2*, lesson 10; *Primary 4*, lesson 37).

• I can receive answers to my prayers (D&C 8:2; *Primary 2*, lesson 18; *Primary 4*, lesson 9).

• I can learn more about Jesus and His commandments as I read the scriptures (2 Nephi 32:3; *Primary 1*, lesson 41; *Primary 6*, lesson 37).

• As I follow Jesus, my faith grows (2 Nephi 31:10; *Primary 2*, lesson 15; *Primary 4*, lesson 22).

• Heavenly Father answers our prayers in different ways (*Primary 2*, lesson 18).

• Quote: "As we pray, we should think of our Heavenly Father as being close by; full of knowledge, understanding, love, and compassion; the essence of power." - President James E. Faust, Second Counselor in the First Presidency (*Ensign*, January 1999, page 2).

• See More Teaching Tools (Theme 7) previewed in the back of this book, available in the *Primary Partners® Teaching Tools—I Belong to The Church of Jesus Christ of Latter-day Saints* book or CD-ROM (to print images in color or black & white).

ACTIVITY: I'll Follow Him in Faith (Anytime, Anywhere Prayer True Storyboard)

OBJECTIVE: Read true stories on prayer to help children know that they don't need to be by their bedside to pray; they can pray anytime, and anywhere to seek Heavenly Father's guidance.

TO MAKE VISUALS: *Copy, color, cut out, and laminate the *Anytime, Anywhere Prayer* poster-board parts A-C and visuals (pp. 63-68). Mount parts A-C on a poster and laminate the entire poster.

AHEAD OF TIME: Obtain the following stories from the Internet: www.LDS.org. From the Gospel Library you can go to HTML to obtain the articles. An easy way is to type in *The Friend* in the first box and the story title and author in the second box. To obtain the *Primary 6* Manual lesson 6, from the Gospel Library click on Primary, Manual, 6, and then scroll to the lesson.

THE IMAGES THAT MATCH THE STORIES (shown on the storyboard, right) are listed by the stories as follows: •**Horse:** "Whoa, Blaze!," by Ken Barker, *The Friend*, June 2002, p. 38-40. • **Ducks:** "Alan's Miracle," by Judy Arrington, *The Friend*, April 2001, p. 8. •**Car:** "Trust in the Lord," by Robin B. Lambert, *The Friend*, September 1999, p. 40. •**Fire:** "Fire on the Mountain," by Lloyd H. Parry, *The Friend*, Nov. 1995, p. 8. •**Mosquito:** "The Power of Prayer," Elder L. Edward Brown of the Seventy, *The Friend*, June 2002, p. 9. •**Train:** "Did Teacher Say That I Could?" by Janine Mickelson, *The Friend*, Jan. 2001, p. 18. •**Boy's Shoe Caught in Track:** "Karolina's Prayer," in the *Primary 3 Manual*, lesson 26, pp. 123-124.

TO PRESENT: (1) Ahead of time assign the above prayer stories to teachers to read the story or tell in their own words. (2) Have a child from each class come up with their teacher to post the picture on the storyboard before the story is told.

4 ye R all the 👦👧👦 of God by faith in 🧔 Jesus Christ.

Galatians 3:26

Cut carefully along the inside of the dotted line.

Cut carefully along the inside of the dotted line.

where Prayer

Do not cut along the dotted line. Use this margin to mount the other side.

Cut carefully along the inside of the dotted line.

← Cut carefully along the inside of the dotted line. ←

Do not cut. Use this margin to mount the other side.

Do not cut along the dotted line. Use this margin to mount the other side.

Theme 8   I'll Honor His Name

BITE-SIZE MEMORIZE

There is no other name given whereby salvation cometh.

Mosiah 5:8

SCRIPTURE TO MEMORIZE: Memorize the Mosiah 5:8 Bite-size Memorize poster on page 70 (shown right). Print small posters to hand out to children from the CD-ROM.*

SONG: Sing "Choose the Right Way," *Children's Songbook,* p. 160. This song is illustrated in *Primary Partners® Singing Fun!—I Belong to The Church of Jesus Christ of Latter-day Saints* book and CD-ROM.

LESSON: Ask, "How can we honor the name of Jesus Christ and Heavenly Father?" Answer the questions using the scriptures, Primary lessons, and sources below to teach.

• I take the name of Jesus Christ upon me when I am baptized (D&C 18:22; 20:37; *Primary 4,* lessons 10, 12).

• When I take the sacrament, I renew my baptismal covenants: I promise to keep the Lord's commandments and always remember Him (D&C 20:77, 79; *Primary 3,* lesson 32, 33).

• I will use the names of Heavenly Father and Jesus reverently (Exodus 20:7; *Primary 3,* lesson 43).

• See More Teaching Tools (Theme 8) previewed in the back of this book, available in the *Primary Partners® Teaching Tools—I Belong to The Church of Jesus Christ of Latter-day Saints* book or CD-ROM (to print images in color or black & white).

ACTIVITY: I'll Honor His Name (Children Around the World Honor Jesus)

OBJECTIVE: Help children look at different situations and try to guess how the people in these stories honored Jesus.

TO MAKE VISUALS: *Copy, color, and laminate the children and situations (pages 71-77) and the world (pages 10-11 used for Theme 1 presentation). Post the world on a poster or board. Place double-stick tape on the back of each picture of a child to mount on the board.

TO PRESENT: Assign teachers or older children ahead of time to read the situation story. Post the world on the board. Have children who are reading come up one at a time and post their child on the board around the world. Then read their story, stopping after they read, "WHAT DO YOU THINK _____ DID TO HONOR JESUS?" Children can raise their hand and answer. Then have the child who is reading read what that child in the story did to honor Jesus.

There is no other name given whereby salvation cometh.

Mosiah 5:8

Jennifer

AMERICA:

Jennifer saved money for a new dolly. Even though she loved the little rag doll her grandmother made her, her old dolly, Dottie, was worn out. Her dress needed mending and her hair was falling out. Sunday, the bishop had announced a new temple was going to be built in their city and he asked the members to contribute money to build the temple. **WHAT DO YOU THINK JENNIFER DID TO HONOR JESUS' NAME?** —Jennifer was so excited about the beautiful new temple and felt her heart swell because she knew what she should do. The next Sunday she happily gave the bishop all the money she had saved for her new doll. Every time she looked at her old dolly she remembered the temple and it made Dottie seem even more precious to her. **JENNIFER HONORED JESUS BY GIVING WHAT SHE HAD TO BUILD UP THE KINGDOM OF GOD.**

Dimitri

RUSSIAN:

Dimitri loved school and had many friends there. Some were boys and girls from his Primary, but there were others who belonged to other religions. He liked them all. But some of his friends said words that made him feel uncomfortable, words they heard on television or in the movies. Dimitri wanted his friends to like him so he felt pressured to repeat some of the bad language. He thought it might help them like him better.

WHAT DO YOU THINK DIMITRI DID TO HONOR JESUS' NAME?

—He decided that he would honor Jesus by always saying good words, even if his friends chose differently. He felt peace because he knew it was the right thing to do.

DIMITRI HONORED JESUS BY CHOOSING TO SAY RESPECTFUL WORDS.

Sharla

FRANCE:

Sharla worked at a flower shop after school to earn extra francs (money). This week she was saving to buy a new outfit for an upcoming party. She has just been paid. It felt good to have the francs in her pocket. That day at work she was carefully clipping the thorns off the roses and grouping them into a bouquet when she saw a small boy looking at the roses. She could see that he couldn't afford to buy them, but she started talking to him anyway. He said his grandmother was very sick and that she loved roses. As the boy walked away, Sharla thought about what he said and about the outfit she wanted.

WHAT DO YOU THINK SHARLA DID TO HONOR JESUS' NAME?

—As Sharla saw the boy go around the corner she dropped a thorny rose and raced to catch up with him. She said, "Come over here I have a surprise for your grandmother." Handing him a rose bouquet she said, "It's free. I have some extra money so let me help you cheer her up. These are the best roses we have." Sharla paid for them, knowing how happy the boy's grandmother would be to see the beautiful flowers.

SHARLA HONORED JESUS BY SHARING AND CARING FOR OTHERS.

Shaka

AFRICA:

Shaka's favorite time with his dad was caring for their animals and birds in a refuge they had made in Africa. They spent hours caring for the creatures they had found that were injured in the jungle. People would bring in animals and birds to have them cared for. His dad was a vet, so he could fix broken legs and cuts and more. Most of the time the animals were tied up, in cages, or fenced-in until they could get well. Then his dad would take them back into the jungle. One day Shaka's friends wanted to let one of the injured birds out of the cage to see if it could fly. They wanted to take it to a cliff and let it go.

WHAT DO YOU THINK SHAKA DID TO HONOR JESUS?

—Shaka grabbed the bird's cage and ran towards his dad to help protect the bird. He knew that only his dad could say if the bird was ready to fly. His friends walked away. Shaka felt happy that he had protected this tiny bird.

SHAKA HONORED JESUS BY SHOWING RESPECT FOR HEAVENLY FATHER'S CREATIONS.

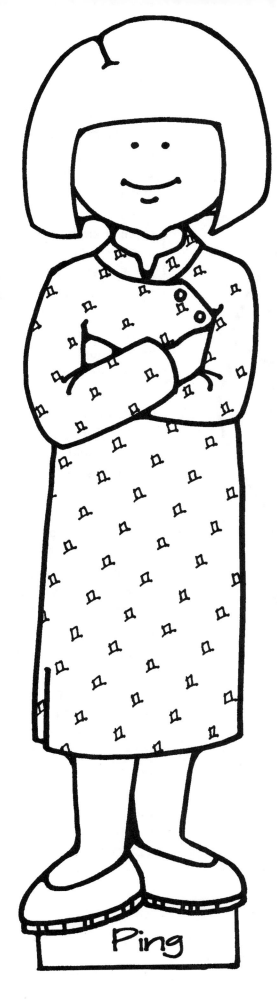

Ping

CHINESE:

It was Saturday morning and Ping's Primary teacher was taking them to the Hong Kong Temple grounds. She was so excited to put on her best dress and go with her friends. When she got to the church Ping was smiling. On the way there they sang "I Love to See the Temple." This made Ping want to go even more. On the temple grounds their teacher asked them to sit on the grass and look up. The teacher started telling about the temple when a boy sitting next to Ping said, "Let's go run through the flowers." Ping remembered the picture of Jesus hanging in her room and wondered what Jesus would do.

WHAT DID PING DO TO HONOR JESUS?

—Ping got up from where she was sitting and moved to the front where she could hear her teacher. She listened carefully to what she was saying and asked questions. She felt so happy that she was at this sacred place where she chose to listen.

PING HONORED JESUS BY BEING REVERENT AT HEAVENLY FATHER'S HOUSE.

Scotty

AUSTRALIA:

Scotty loved the giant cookies his mother made for him and his brother Jayson. One Saturday, Scotty saw his mother making their favorite cookies. Soon Scotty could smell them baking. His mother called, "Come and get it." This day the cookies seemed especially good. He had missed the cookies his mother baked last week while he was gone fishing. Scotty ate his so fast that he looked around for another bite and it was all gone. He asked his mother for another and she said he could only have one or he would spoil his appetite for dinner. He still had a sweet tooth as he looked at his brother's cookie. Jayson hadn't come in to eat his yet, so Scotty was tempted to eat Jayson's cookie.

WHAT DID SCOTTY DO TO HONOR JESUS?
—Scotty carefully put Jayson's cookie in a bag so he wouldn't be tempted and asked his mother to put it away until his brother Jayson came in. Scotty felt relieved that he cared enough for his brother to save his cookie. **SCOTTY HONORED JESUS BY SHOWING RESPECT FOR OTHERS.**

Maria

MEXICO:

Maria had beautiful hair and she loved taking care of it every day. Today was special as she was going to a fiesta where they would have a picnic, dance, and break a piñata filled with candy and small toys. She hoped they would notice the pretty comb she wore in her hair as they blindfolded her to hit the piñata. Her mother helped her glue silk flowers on the comb to match her dress. As she stood in line for the piñata, Rosa, a girl from school, came up behind her. Rosa's hair was uncombed and she didn't even have a pretty dress to wear. Maria knew that she came from a family that had very little money.

WHAT DO YOU THINK MARIA DID TO HONOR JESUS' NAME?

—Rosa told Maria that she didn't have time to comb her hair, so Maria took the pretty comb out of her hair and used it to comb Rosa's hair. Before they got to the head of the line, Maria had carefully placed the comb in her friend's hair. This made her feel proud that Rosa could feel and look pretty too.

MARIA HONORED JESUS BY LOVING AND CARING FOR OTHERS.

Theme 9   I'll Do What is Right

Thou [shalt] do t[hat] which is [right]... in the [eyes] of the Lord.

Deuteronomy 6:18

SCRIPTURE TO MEMORIZE: Memorize the Deuteronomy 6:18 Bite-size Memorize poster on page 79 (shown left). Print small posters to hand out to children from the CD-ROM.*

SONG: Sing "Kindness Begins with Me," *Children's Songbook*, p. 145.

LESSON: Ask, "What choices do we make when we do what is right?" Answer the questions using the scriptures, Primary lessons, and sources below.

• I can know when the Holy Ghost is helping me choose the right (Moroni 10:5; *Primary 3*, lesson 26; *Primary 6*, lesson 27).

• Choose one or two of the principles from *My Gospel Standards* to present each week. *My Gospel Standards* are found in the *Primary 6 Old Testament Manual*, lesson 47, pages 215-216 or in *My Achievement Days* booklet [35317], back cover. Gospel standard principles to present: I am a child of God, Heavenly Father loves us and we can love Him, pray to Heavenly Father, follow Jesus, remember baptismal covenants and listen to the Holy Ghost, be honest, seek good friends and treat others kindly, dress modestly, read and watch things that are pleasing to Heavenly Father, listen to music that is pleasing to Heavenly Father, keep mind and body sacred and pure and not partake of harmful things, keep Sabbath day holy, choose the right and repent, live to be worthy to serve a mission and go to the temple, and follow Heavenly Father's plan.

• See More Teaching Tools (Theme 9) previewed in the back of this book, available in the *Primary Partners® Teaching Tools—I Belong to The Church of Jesus Christ of Latter-day Saints* book or CD-ROM (to print images in color or black & white).

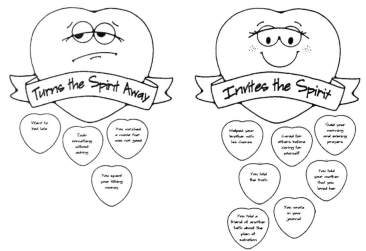

Turns the Spirit Away

Invites the Spirit

ACTIVITY: The Holy Ghost Will Guide Me (Invite the Spirit Choices Game)

OBJECTIVE: Help children learn to make choices that invite the Spirit of the Holy Ghost.

TO MAKE VISUALS: *Copy, color, cut out, and laminate visuals (pages 80-85). The hearts can be mounted on two separate posters or on the board. Place heart wordstrips in a container.

TO PRESENT: Post the two large hearts and explain, "Our choices can either invite the Spirit of the Holy Ghost or turn the Spirit away. If we invite the Spirit we can be guided, warned, or comforted. If we do wrong, we can't expect the Spirit to help us. We do not have to hear an actual voice; we may have a strong feeling about something. When this happens we need to obey."

To Play: Have children take turns drawing a heart wordstrip from the container and reading it aloud. Tape the heart wordstrip below the heart it matches: "Invites the Spirit," or "Turns the Spirit Away." If they draw a wordstrip that reads "Invites the Spirit?" or "Turns the Spirit Away?" have them tell something someone might do to invite the Spirit or turn the Spirit away. *Option:* Have children softly say, "yea!" if the action invites the spirit or "no!" if it turns the spirit away. Or they can silently do thumbs up or thumbs down to vote on the action. **Additional Activity:** At the end of the activity, if there is time, have children draw wordstrips and have them pantomime the actions to have children guess what they are, and then vote which ones invite the Spirit and the ones that turn the Spirit away.

*All images can be printed in full color or black and white using the CD-ROM:
Primary Partners Sharing Time—I Belong to The Church of Jesus Christ of Latter-day Saints.

78

Thou shalt do that which is right ... in the sight of the Lord.

Deuteronomy 6:18

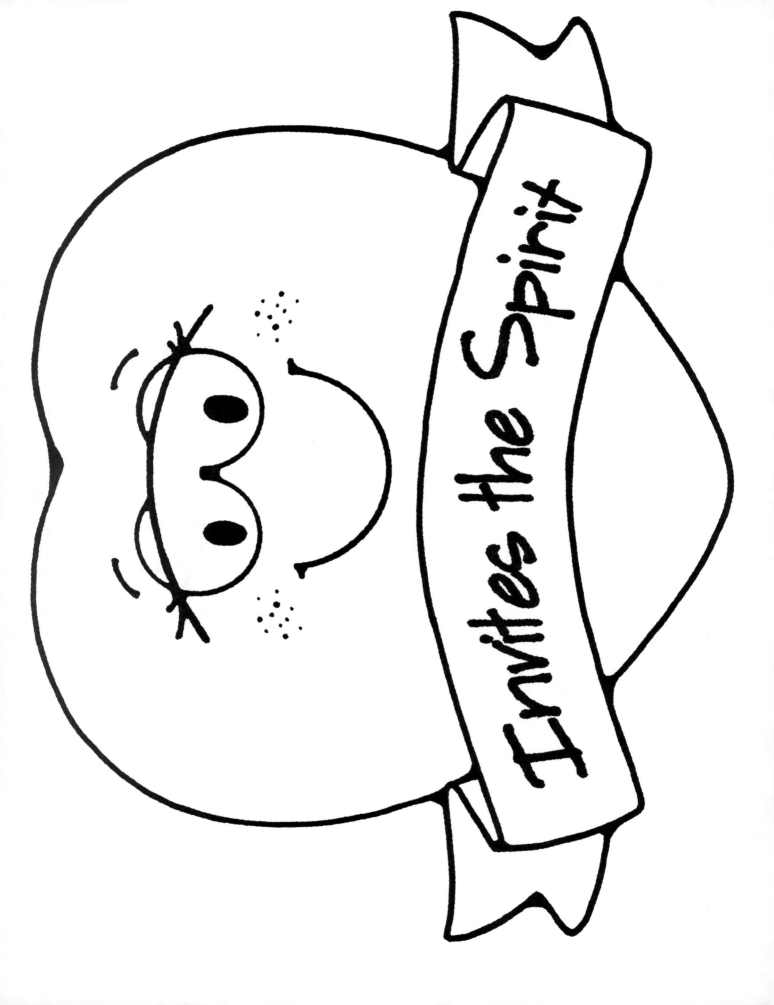

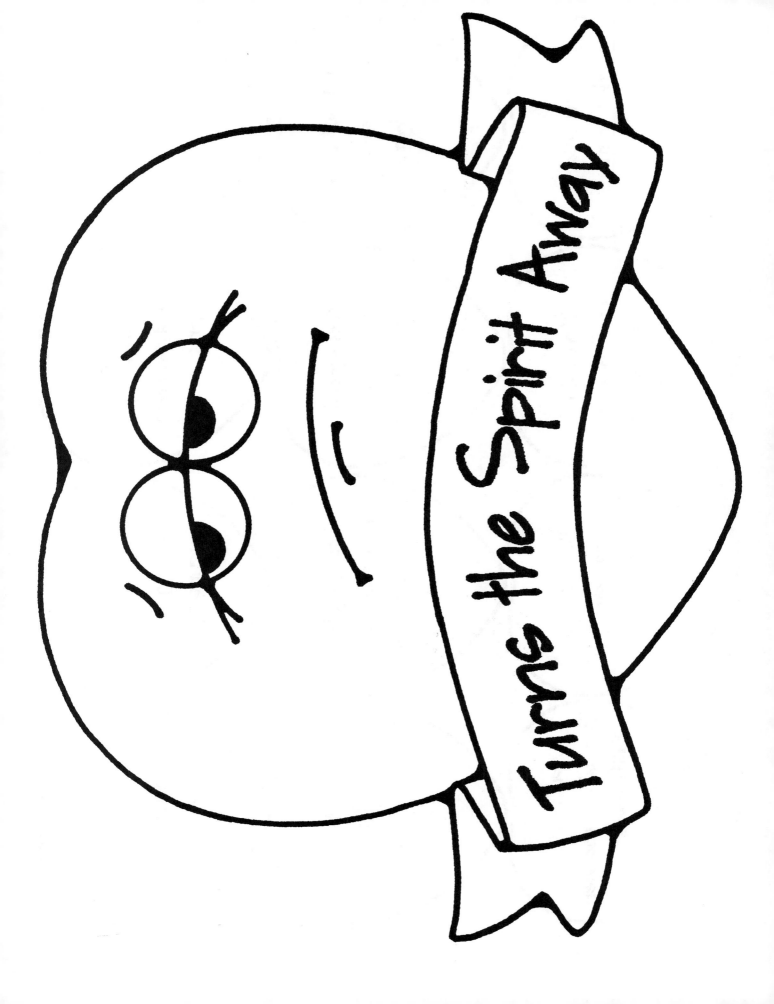

You told
the truth

Helped your
brother with
his chores

Went to
bed late

You told
your mother
that you
loved her

You spent
your tithing
money

Said your
morning
and evening
prayers

You wrote
in your
journal

You watched
a movie that
was not good

Cared for
others before
caring for
yourself

You told a
friend of another
faith about the
plan of
salvation

You told
a lie

Took
something
without
asking

Said you would
fast but ate
breakfast
anyway

Was reverent
in Primary

Searched
the
scriptures

Was angry
when your
mother asked
you to help

Got even
when someone
hurt your
feelings

You were
feeling good but
said you
were sick

Disobeyed
your father

Smoked a
cigarette to
be cool

Visited and
cheered up
a lonely
friend

Didn't go
straight home
and didn't
call your
mother

Prayed for
a friend
who needed
special help

Thanked your
teacher for
teaching

Took out the garbage without being asked

You were polite even though someone else was rude

Invites the Spirit ?

You were forgiving and kind

Said a swear word when you were mad

Invites the Spirit ?

You enjoyed learning how to do your geneology

Gave someone a hug

Invites the Spirit ?

Said something unkind about a friend

Borrowed a pen and didn't return it

Invites the Spirit ?

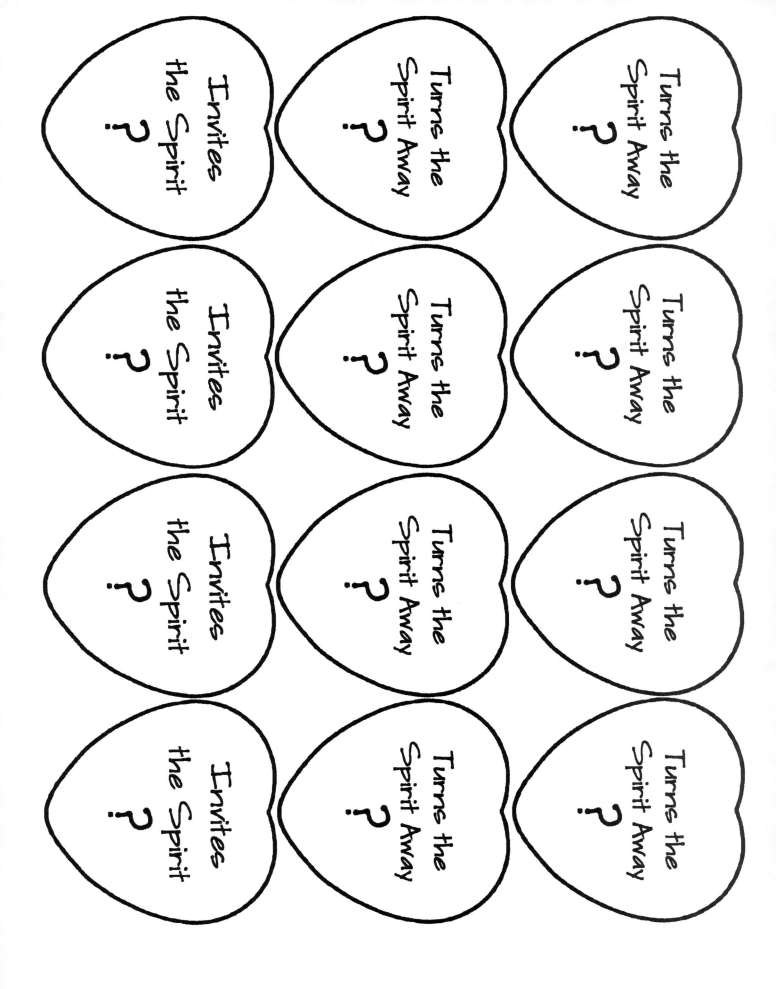

Theme 10   I'll Follow His Light

SCRIPTURE TO MEMORIZE: Memorize the John 14:6 Bite-size Memorize poster on page 87 (shown left). Print small posters to hand out to children from the CD-ROM.*

SONGS: Sing "Tell Me the Stories of Jesus," p. 57, "Shine On," page 144, and "Keep the Commandments," page 146, from the *Children's Songbook*.

LESSON: Ask, "How can we follow Jesus who is our light?" Answer the questions using the scriptures, Primary lessons, and sources below to teach.

• Jesus lights the way as my example (3 Nephi 18:16).

• Jesus lights the ways with His teachings (D&C 84:45-46; *Primary 7*, lessons 10, 12).

• I will follow His light and be an example (3 Nephi 18:24; *Primary 1*, lesson 36; *Primary 2*, lesson 29).

• As I follow His light, I am protected (Psalm 27:1; *Primary 4*, lessons 25, 26).

• See *New Testament Stories*

• See More Teaching Tools (Theme 10) previewed in the back of this book, available in the *Primary Partners® Teaching Tools—I Belong to The Church of Jesus Christ of Latter-day Saints* book or CD-ROM (to print images in color or black & white).

ACTIVITY: I Will Follow Jesus Christ (Facing the Sun/Son Stories of Jesus)

OBJECTIVE: Help children know the importance of following Jesus Christ, the Son of God, to help our testimonies grow, just as the sunflowers face the sun to grow.

TO MAKE VISUALS: *Copy, color, cut out, and laminate visuals (pages 88-94). Cut out the stories.

TO PRESENT:

1. Post one sunflower on the board and say, "When the sun comes up in the morning, the sunflowers turn their face toward the sun. The sunflowers need the warmth of the sun to grow. When the sun travels through the sky the sunflowers turn their heads to follow the sun."

2. Post Jesus on the board and say, "We too can face the Son of God (Jesus Christ) to help our testimonies grow. Each day we can read the scriptures to learn about the life of Jesus Christ and the stories He taught. We can follow Jesus Christ by living His commandments. The Apostles of Jesus Christ looked to Him to learn of the commandments and how they should live. They testify of Jesus Christ in the scriptures and we can learn of Him by reading their words. Let's learn of the stories of Jesus written by the Apostles to learn how we can follow Him."

3. Tell children, "These are the stories Jesus taught. Let's read them to learn how we can follow His light." To present the stories, have children take turns drawing sunflowers from the container. The leaders or older children could read the stories and post the sunflower around the Jesus sun. Talk about each story and how you can follow the Son of God (Jesus Christ).

*All images can be printed in full color or black and white using the CD-ROM:
Primary Partners Sharing Time—I Belong to The Church of Jesus Christ of Latter-day Saints.

86

I am the way, the truth, and the life: no man cometh N2 the Father, but by me.

John 14:6

Do not cut along the dotted line. Use this margin to mount the other side.

Cut carefully along the inside of the dotted line.

THE GOOD SAMARITAN: Jesus told the story of a Jew who was beaten by thieves who took his clothes. They left him almost dead. First a Jewish priest and then another Jewish man saw him but passed by. Then a Samaritan came and put clothes on him and took him to an inn, giving him money so he could get well. The Samaritan was a good neighbor. **I CAN BE KIND AND SERVE OTHERS.**

THE WIDOW'S MITES: Jesus was by the temple watching people give money to the Church. Many rich men put a lot of money into the boxes. Then a poor widow woman came to the box. Her husband had died. She put in two pieces of money called mites. Two mites were not very much money, but they were all she had. Jesus saw her and taught His disciples a lesson. The rich men gave a lot of money, but they had more money at home. But the widow had only two mites with no money at home, and she gave all her money to the Church. She had given more to the Church than all of the rich men. **I CAN PAY TITHES AND OFFERINGS.**

THE LOST SHEEP: A good shepherd had 100 sheep and one was lost. The shepherd left the other 99 sheep to look for the lost one to save it from the wolves and from hunger. He found it, picked it up and put it on his shoulders to carry it home. Jesus is the Good Shepherd and He is happy when sinners (who are lost) repent. **I CAN FIND AND HELP THOSE IN NEED.**

THE LOST SON: A man had two sons who would receive money when he died. The younger son asked for his share of the money now. Receiving the money he went to another land. Because he spent his money foolishly, he had no money to buy food. He became so hungry he wanted to eat the pigs' food. He decided to go home and ask to be a servant in his father's house and repent. His father ran to him, threw his arms around him and kissed him, clothed him, put a ring on his finger, and fed him. This story shows that Jesus loves everyone and wants us to repent and return to His presence. **I CAN LOVE AND FORGIVE OTHERS.**

THE TEN LEPERS: Jesus saw ten sick men in a small town. They were lepers who had sores all over their bodies and their skin was falling off. People did not want to be near them because they could get sick too, and doctors could not help them. The lepers asked Jesus to heal them, to make their sores go away. Jesus told them to go to the priests and they obeyed. On their way Jesus healed them and their sores were gone. One of the lepers came back, knelt down, and thanked Jesus for making him well. The other nine lepers did not come back to thank Jesus. Jesus told the leper that his faith made him well. **I CAN SHOW GRATITUDE TOWARD OTHERS.**

THE TALENTS: Jesus told the story of a man who was going to another land. Before he went, he gave his servants talents (money). To the first he gave five talents. This servant worked hard and made five more talents and then he had ten talents. The second servant was given two talents. He worked hard and made two more talents and then he had four talents. To the third servant he gave one talent. This servant buried his one talent in the ground, afraid he would lose it. He did not make any more talents. When the man came home, he asked his servants what they had done with their talents. He rewarded the servant who made ten talents by making him a leader over many things, telling him to be happy. He gave the second servant two more talents and made him a leader. The servant who buried his talent was lazy, so the leader took his one talent away from him and gave it to the servant who made ten talents. **I CAN WORK TO INCREASE MY TALENTS.**

TEN YOUNG WOMEN: Ten young women went to a wedding, waiting at the door for the bridegroom to let them in. No one knew when the bridegroom would let them in. All ten of the women's lamps burned oil, but only five were wise and brought extra oil to keep their lamps burning. When the foolish young women discovered they did not have enough oil to keep their lamps burning they left to buy more oil. While they were gone, the bridegroom came and let the five wise women in the door to go to the wedding. The other five came back and the door was closed. They could not go to the wedding. The bridegroom is Jesus who will come to the earth again and we must be ready. **I CAN BE PREPARED FOR THE SECOND COMING.**

THE RICH YOUNG MAN: A rich young man asked Jesus what he should do to get to heaven. Jesus told him to obey God's commandments. The young man said he obeyed the commandments. Jesus asked him to do one more thing and sell everything he had, give the money to the poor, and follow Jesus. Then he could go to heaven. The young man was sad and went away. He loved his money more than he loved God. Jesus told His disciples it is hard for a rich man who loves riches to go to heaven. **I CAN GIVE TO THE POOR AND NEEDY.**

Theme 11   Teachings of the Prophet

SCRIPTURE TO MEMORIZE: Memorize the Amos 3:7 Bite-size Memorize poster on page 96 (shown right). Print small posters to hand out to children from the CD-ROM.*

SONGS: Sing "Remember the Sabbath," p. 155 and "Follow the Prophet," page 110 in the *Children's Songbook.*

LESSON: During this month help the children understand the blessings that come from obeying the prophet's counsel given at general conference. Help them to apply the messages in their lives and share the messages with their families. Choose scriptures, songs, and class manual references that reinforce the messages.

• See More Teaching Tools (Theme 11) previewed in the back of this book, available in the *Primary Partners® Teaching Tools—I Belong to The Church of Jesus Christ of Latter-day Saints* book or CD-ROM (to print images in color or black & white).

ACTIVITY: I Am Blessed When I Follow the Prophet (Blessings Brainstorm)

OBJECTIVE: Help children view images that remind them of ways they can follow the prophet and the blessings that come from following him.

TO MAKE VISUALS: *Copy, color, cut out, and laminate visuals (pages 97-100). Cut out the wordstrips and place on the back of each visual to help children identify them.

TO PRESENT: Ahead of time, hide the visuals around the room, making a map as a reminder of where they were placed. Tell children that they are blessed in may ways as they follow the prophet. Help them find ways we can follow the prophet and think of ways we are blessed when we follow him. Have children take turns finding a visual. As they walk you can tell them they are getting warmer as they approach the visual or colder as they are far away. When they find the visual have them post it on the board and say what the visual represents, e.g., a carrot reminds us that a prophet has asked us to plant a garden. Have the child tell why planting a garden will bring us blessings, e.g.: Planting a garden blesses us with food to eat in times of need.

Reference: The following quotes found on the visuals above are from prophets and an Apostle:
• "Write in your journal each day" (Prophet Spencer W. Kimball). • "Keep the Word of Wisdom" (Prophet Heber J. Grant). • "Find friends that choose the right" (Apostle Robert D. Hales). • "Believe in Jesus Christ" (Prophet Joseph Fielding Smith). • "Be a missionary" (Prophet David O. McKay). • "Learn to work at home and do a job well" (Prophet Ezra Taft Benson). • "Respect your parents" (Prophet Gordon B. Hinckley). • "Smile and be kind to others" (Prophet David O. McKay). • "Be a friend to the friendless" (Prophet George Albert Smith). • "Plant a garden" (Prophet Spencer W. Kimball). • "Read and study the Book of Mormon" (Prophet Ezra Taft Benson). "Pay your tithing" (Prophet Lorenzo Snow).

Surely the Lord God do nothing, but he revealeth his secret N2 his serv the prophets.

Amos 3:7

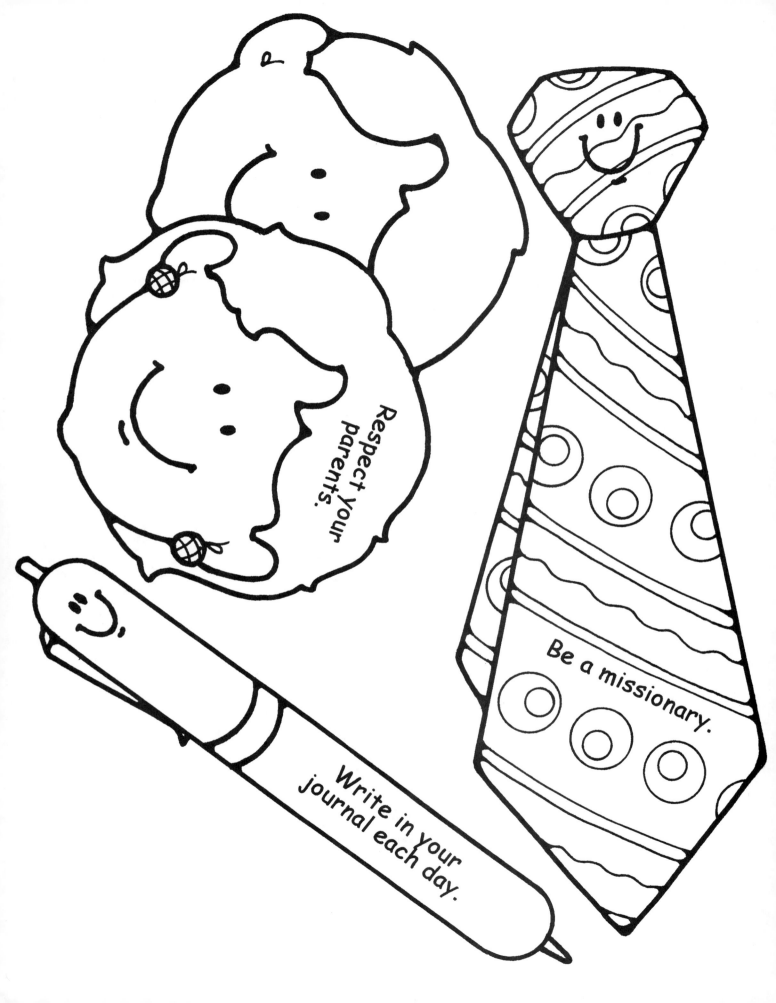

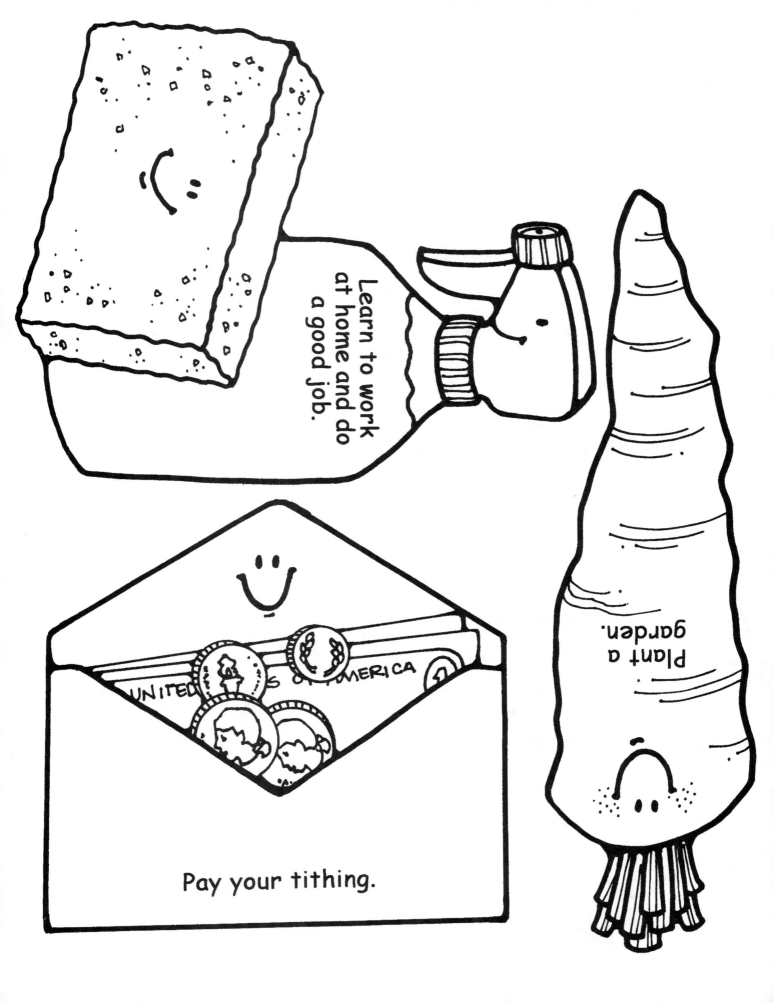

Learn to work at home and do a good job.

Plant a garden.

Pay your tithing.

Keep the Word of Wisdom.

Find friends that choose the right.

Be a friend to the friendless.

Theme 12   His Truth I Will Proclaim

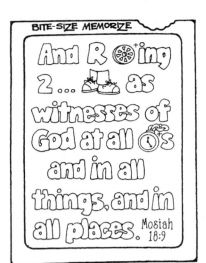

SCRIPTURE TO MEMORIZE: Memorize the Mosiah 18:9 Bite-size Memorize poster on page 102 (shown right). Print small posters to hand out to children from the CD-ROM.*

SONG: Sing "I Want to Be a Missionary Now," p. 168, and "We'll Bring the World His Truth," page 172, in the *Children's Songbook.*

LESSON: Ask, "How can we share the truth of the gospel with others?" Answer the questions using the scriptures, Primary lessons, and sources below.

• What is a testimony? I can have a testimony of Jesus Christ, His gospel, and His Church (D&C 76:22; *Primary 4*, lessons 33, 44; *Primary 5*, lesson 46).

• I can share the gladness of the gospel with others (D&C 84:62; *Primary 2*, lesson 11; *Primary 4*, lesson 17).

• I can prepare to be a missionary now (1 Timothy 4:12; *Primary 3*, lesson 25; *Primary 6*, lesson 9).

• I am grateful for the Savior and the blessings of my membership in His Church (Mosiah 2:41; *Primary 1*, lesson 42; *Primary 3*, lesson 21).

• See More Teaching Tools (Theme 12) previewed in the back of this book, available in the *Primary Partners® Teaching Tools—I Belong to The Church of Jesus Christ of Latter-day Saints* book or CD-ROM (to print images in color or black & white).

ACTIVITY: I Will Share My Testimony of the Gospel (Stand as a Witness Testimony Time)

OBJECTIVE: Encourage children to think about and bear their testimony of specific gospel subjects.

TO MAKE VISUALS: *Copy, color, and cut out the *I Stand as a Witness* sign parts A and B and cards (pages 103-108). Mount the sign on a poster and laminate the entire poster. Laminate the cards and place in a container.

TO PRESENT: Tell children that they can stand as a witness of Jesus Christ and testify of His gospel anytime and anywhere. Whenever they feel inspired or have the opportunity they can share their testimony of the gospel with others. Your testimony grows as you learn about the gospel and try to live its principles each day. The prophet and his Apostles stand as a witness of Jesus Christ every day and so can we.

Testimony Time: Have children come up one at a time to draw a *Testimony Time* card from the container. Ask them to post the card on the board or poster and bear their testimony, telling how they feel about the subject on the card. Or, they can teach like a missionary, telling everything they know about the subject.

*All images can be printed in full color or black and white using the CD-ROM:
Primary Partners Sharing Time—I Belong to The Church of Jesus Christ of Latter-day Saints.

And R◎ing 2 ... 👟 as witnesses of God at all ⏰S and in all things, and in all places. Mosiah 18:9

Cut carefully along the inside of the dotted line.

STAND AS

A WITNESS

← Do not cut along the dotted line. Use this margin to mount the other side.

Book of Mormon

Word of Wisdom

Plan of Salvation

Missionary Work

Temples

Prophet

Family

Jesus Christ

HOLY GHOST

PRAYER

BAPTISM

TITHING

Repentance

Marriage

Joseph Smith

Priesthood

More Teaching Tools

The following Teaching Tools suggest more ideas for Sharing Time for
Themes 1-12 "I Belong to The Church of Jesus Christ of Latter-day Saints" 2003 year.

We have made it easier for you to access all of the following Teaching Tools
without purchasing the following eight *Primary Partners* activity books and CD-ROMs
(that coordinate with the *Primary 1-7 Manuals*):
Primary Partners Nursery and Age 3, Volume 1 and 2
Primary Partners CTR-A and *Primary Partners CTR-B*
Primary Partners Ages 8-12 New Testament, Old Testament,
Book of Mormon, and Doctrine and Covenants and Church History

We have combined all of the Teaching Tools suggested on the following pages
in one book and CD-ROM with full-color or black and white images.

To use the following Teaching Tools, simply copy the activities found in
the <u>eight</u> *Primary Partners* books (listed above), or the <u>one</u> *Primary
Partners Teaching Tools* book and CD-ROM (shown above):

• For large sharing time groups, enlarge the activities to show-and-tell.

Theme 1:   I Belong to The Church of Jesus Christ - 3 Nephi 26:21

- **Heavenly Father Loves and Blesses Us. He Sent His Son, Jesus Christ to Earth to Be Our Savior**
(John 3:16; *Primary 1*, lesson 6; *Primary 6*, lesson 2).

I CHOSE TO FOLLOW JESUS Premortal Life Puppet Show in the *Primary Partners CTR-A* book or CD-ROM (lesson 4).

MY FAITH GROWS AS I OBEY Premortal Life, Earth-life Quiz in the *Primary Partners Doctrine and Covenants* book or CD-ROM (lesson 28).

THE MISSION OF JESUS CHRIST Review Game in the *Primary Partners New Testament* book or CD-ROM (lesson 35).

- **Jesus Organized His Church. He Ordained Others to the Priesthood to Act in His Name**
(Matthew 16:19; *Primary 7*, lesson 15).
- **The New Testament Teaches Us about Christ's Church**
(Articles of Faith 1:6; *Primary 7*, lesson 9; *Gospel Principles*, chapter 16).
- **When People Began to Change Jesus' Teachings, Many Fell Away from His Church (Apostasy). The Apostles Were Killed, and the Lord Withdrew His Priesthood Authority**
(Joseph Smith—History 1:19; D&C 1:15; *Primary 5*, lesson 2).

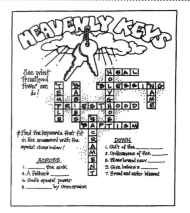

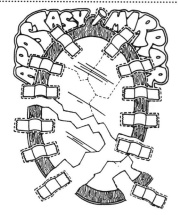

HEAVENLY KEYS Priesthood Keys Crossword Puzzle (shown left) in the *Primary Partners New Testament* book or CD-ROM (lesson 15).

JESUS CHRIST'S CHURCH IS RESTORED Apostles Mirror Puzzle Teaching Tool in the *Primary Partners Doctrine and Covenants* book or CD-ROM (lesson 2).

THE APOSTLES WERE SPECIAL WITNESSES OF JESUS CHRIST Apostle Match Game in the *Primary Partners New Testament* book or CD-ROM (lesson 9).

Copy the above images from the *Primary Partners Teaching Tools-I Belong to The Church of Jesus Christ of Latter-day Saints* book, or print in color or black & white from the CD-ROM. Or, copy or print the images from the corresponding *Primary Partners* books or CD-ROMs.

Theme 2:   I Belong to The Church of Jesus Christ – D&C 115:4

- In the First Vision, Joseph Smith Saw God the Father and His Son, Jesus Christ. He Learned That Christ's True Church Would Be Restored in These Latter-days (Articles of Faith 1:1, 6; Joseph Smith—History 1:7-20; *Primary 5,* lesson 1.
- Joseph Smith Was Called to Be a Prophet. He Translated the Book of Mormon, Which Contains the Fulness of the Gospel (Articles of Faith 1:8; D&C 124:125; *Primary 3,* lesson 15).
- The Priesthood, Ordinances, and Doctrines Were Restored by Heavenly Messengers and Revelation (Articles of Faith 1:5, 9; D&C 13:1; *Primary 5,* lessons 8, 12).

JOSEPH SMITH SAW HEAVENLY FATHER AND JESUS Sacred Grove Moveable Scene in the *Primary Partners CTR-B* book or CD-ROM (lesson 5).

THE PRIESTHOOD BLESSES MY LIFE Priesthood Pockets Puzzle the *Primary Partners Old Testament* book or CD-ROM (lesson 33).

FULNESS OF THE GOSPEL—ANGEL MORONI'S GOOD NEWS MESSAGE Moroni's Match Game the *Primary Partners Doctrine and Covenants* book or CD-ROM (lesson 3).

- The Priesthood, Ordinances, and Doctrines Were Restored by Heavenly Messengers and Revelation (Articles of Faith 1:5, 9; D&C 13:1; *Primary 5,* lessons 8, 12).
- We Make and Keep Covenants When We Become Members of the Church (D&C 136:4; *Primary 3,* lesson 13; *Primary 4,* lesson 12).

PRIESTHOOD ORDINANCES RESTORED Ordinance Opportunity Game in the *Primary Partners Doctrine and Covenants* book or CD-ROM (lesson 12).

THE TRUE CHURCH WAS RESTORED TO THE EARTH Then and Now Match Game in the *Primary Partners Doctrine and Covenants* book or CD-ROM (lesson 11).

JESUS CHRIST'S CHURCH RESTORED Membership Window Wheel in the *Primary Partners CTR-B* book or CD-ROM (lesson 6).

I PROMISE AND HEAVENLY FATHER PROMISES Two-sided Puzzle in the *Primary Partners CTR-B* book or CD-ROM (lesson 13).

Copy the above images from the *Primary Partners Teaching Tools-I Belong to The Church of Jesus Christ of Latter-day Saints* book, or print in color or black & white from the CD-ROM. Or, copy or print the images from the corresponding *Primary Partners* books or CD-ROMs.

Theme 3:   I Know Who I Am — Psalm 82:6

- **I Am a Child of God and Lived in Heaven Before I Came to Earth**
  (D&C 93:29; 76:24; *Primary 2*, lesson 3).
- **I Am a Child of God Blessed with Divine Nature** (3 Nephi 27:27;
  The Family: A Proclamation to the World, paragraphs 1-2; *Primary 1*, lesson 1).
- **I Am a Child of God. He Has Given Me Spiritual Gifts and Talents**
  (Articles of Faith 1:7; D&C 46:11; *Primary 5*, lesson 19).
- **I Am a Child of God. I Will Serve My Family and Others**
  (Mosiah 2:17; *Primary 2*, lesson 39; *Primary 6*, lesson 10, enrichment activities).

I CAN RECOGNIZE AND SEEK TRUE GIFTS Gifts of the Spirit Cross Match in the *Primary Partners Doctrine and Covenants* book or CD-ROM (less. 19).

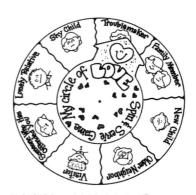

I WILL SHOW LOVE TO OTHERS AS I SERVE My Circle of Love Spin-and-Serve Game in the *Primary Partners Old Testament* book or CD-ROM (less. 10).

I CAN BE HAPPY AS I SERVE Service Station Sack of Reminders in the *Primary Partners Doctrine and Covenants* book or CD-ROM (lesson 39).

I WILL USE MY TALENTS TO SERVE OTHERS Service and Talent Show Poster in the *Primary Partners New Testament* book or CD-ROM (lesson 26).

Copy the above images from the *Primary Partners Teaching Tools-I Belong to The Church of Jesus Christ of Latter-day Saints* book, or print in color or black & white from the CD-ROM. Or, copy or print the images from the corresponding *Primary Partners* books or CD-ROMs.

Theme 4:   I Believe in the Savior, Jesus Christ – Matthew 16:16

- **Jesus Is the Savior of All Mankind. I Have Faith in the Lord Jesus Christ**
  (Articles of Faith 1:4; Mosiah 3:9; *Primary 4*, lesson 43).
- **As I Have Faith, I Want to Repent and Be Baptized**
  (Mosiah 18:10; *Primary 2*, lesson 12; *Primary 4*, lesson 14).

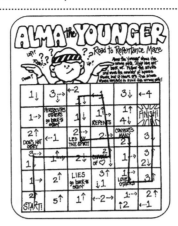

JESUS SUFFERED FOR ME Atonement Ponder Wheel in the *Primary Partners New Testament* book or CD-ROM (lesson 32).

I CAN LIVE IN HEAVEN Alma the Younger's Road to Repentance Maze in the *Primary Partners Book of Mormon* book or CD-ROM (lesson 14).

JESUS HELPED ME OVERCOME SIN AND DEATH Repentance Puzzle in the *Primary Partners New Testament* book or CD-ROM (lesson 30).

- **I Will Receive the Gift of the Holy Ghost**
  (2 Nephi 32:5; *Primary 1*, lesson 7; *Primary 2*, lesson 13).
- **As I Choose the Right Each Day, I Can Return to Heavenly Father**
  (D&C 6:13; *Primary 2*, lesson 14; *Primary 3*, lesson 3).

THE HOLY GHOST WILL GUIDE AND COMFORT ME Invite the Spirit Choice Game in the *Primary Partners Doctrine and Covenants* book or CD-ROM (lesson 7).

HAPPINESS COMES FROM CHOOSING THE RIGHT CTR Happiness Wheel in the *Primary Partners CTR-A* book or CD-ROM (lesson 1).

Theme 5: The Prophet Speaks for the Savior. I Can Follow the Prophet Today — D&C 1:38

- **A Prophet Is a Man Called by Our Father in Heaven to Speak for Him** (Exodus 3:1-6, 9-12; 1 Samuel 3:1-10, 19-20; Moses 6:26-39; Joseph Smith—History 1:11-20; *Primary 1,* lesson 43; *Gospel Principles,* chapter 9.

I KNOW THE PROPHET LIVES Prophet Poster Fold-out Pictures in the *Primary Partners Nursery-Age 3,* Vol. 1 book or CD-ROM (lesson 43).

I WILL LISTEN TO THE PROPHET TO STAY IN THE LIGHT Cycle of History Wheel in the *Primary Partners Book of Mormon* book or CD-ROM (lesson 41).

- **The Living Prophet Is a Special Witness of Jesus Christ. He Bears Testimony of Heavenly Father and Jesus Christ** (D&C 27:12; 1 Nephi 10:5; Jacob 7:11).
- **The Testimony of the Prophet Strengthens My Faith in Jesus Christ and Guides Us in These Latter-days** (Jacob 4:4-5; D&C 76:19-23; examples from conference talks in the *Friend, Ensign,* and *Liahona*).

THE PROPHET SPEAKS AND I LISTEN Revelation Routes in the *Primary Partners Doctrine and Covenants* book or CD-ROM (lesson 15).

PROPHETS TELL ME ABOUT THE LIFE AND MISSION OF JESUS Prophet Poster Presentation in the *Primary Partners Book of Mormon* book or CD-ROM (less. 31).

THE PROPHETS GIVE LATTER-DAY REVELATION Standard Works Think-athon in the *Primary Partners Doctrine and Covenants* book or CD-ROM (lesson 22).

Copy the above images from the *Primary Partners Teaching Tools-I Belong to The Church of Jesus Christ of Latter-day Saints* book, or print in color or black & white from the CD-ROM. Or, copy or print the images from the corresponding *Primary Partners* books or CD-ROMs.

Theme 6:   I Know God's Plan – Moses 1:39

• **Jesus Is My Savior. Because of Him I Can Have Eternal Life**
(Articles of Faith 1:3; *Primary 4*, lesson 45; *Primary 6*, lesson 45).
• **Heavenly Father and Jesus Created the Earth and All Forms of Life.**
I Can Treat the Earth and All Living Things with Respect (3 Nephi 9:15; *Primary 6*, lessons 1, 3).

JESUS GAVE ME IMMORTALITY AND ETERNAL LIFE
Atonement Object Lesson in the *Primary Partners Old Testament* book or CD-ROM (lesson 45).

HEAVENLY FATHER'S PLAN IS FOR ME Plan of Salvation Story Board and Quiz in the *Primary Partners Old Testament* book or CD-ROM (lesson 1).

• **Agency Is a Gift from Heavenly Father As I Choose Between Right and Wrong,**
I Am Accountable (Articles of Faith 1:2; Alma 34:32; *Primary 2*, lesson 5).

HEAVENLY FATHER TRUSTS US TO FOLLOW
Heaven Road Map in the *Primary Partners CTR-B* book or CD-ROM (lesson 2).

HEAVENLY FATHER GAVE ME FREE AGENCY Choices Slap Game in the *Primary Partners CTR-A* book or CD-ROM (lesson 5).

I WILL SHOW HEAVENLY FATHER AND JESUS RESPECT
Respectful Choices Sticker Poster in the *Primary Partners* Review the Attention Activity (page 25) in the *Primary 7 New Testament Manual* (lesson 8).

4a.

Copy the above images from the *Primary Partners Teaching Tools-I Belong to The Church of Jesus Christ of Latter-day Saints* book, or print in color or black & white from the CD-ROM. Or, copy or print the images from the corresponding *Primary Partners* books or CD-ROMs.

● **I Have Been Sent to a Family to Learn to Follow Jesus**
(1 Nephi 1:1; *Primary 2*, lesson 6; *Primary 3*, lesson 28).

Theme #6 . . .

MY TESTIMONY OF JESUS
What Would Jesus Do? in the
*Primary Partners Book of
Mormon* book or CD-ROM
(lesson 8).

I CAN BE LIKE JESUS Compassion
Wheel in the *Primary Partners New
Testament* book or CD-ROM (lesson 13).

**JESUS CHRIST WAS CHOSEN TO
BE MY SAVIOR** Choices and
Consequences Match Game in the
Primary Partners Old Testament book
or CD-ROM (lesson 2).

**I WILL LIVE THE GOSPEL
OF JESUS CHRIST** Faithful
Footsteps Goal Flip Chart in
the *Primary Partners Old
Testament* book or CD-ROM
(lesson 6).

Copy the above images from the *Primary Partners Teaching Tools-I Belong to The Church of Jesus Christ of Latter-day Saints* book,
or print in color or black & white from the CD-ROM. Or, copy or print the images from the corresponding *Primary Partners* books or CD-ROMs.

Theme 7:   I'll Follow Him in Faith — Galatians 3:26

- **I Can Pray to Heavenly Father Anytime, Anywhere. Heavenly Father Answers Our Prayers in Different Ways** (Alma 34:19-27; *Primary 2*, lesson 10; *Primary 4*, lesson 37; *Primary 2*, lesson 18).

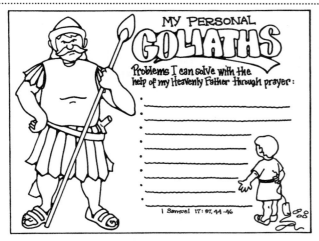

HEAVENLY FATHER HELPS ME AS I PRAY IN FAITH My Personal Goliaths prayer Journal in the *Primary Partners Old Testament* book or CD-ROM (lesson 28).

I WILL SEEK HEAVENLY FATHER'S GUIDANCE Prayer Crossword Puzzle in the *Primary Partners Doctrine & Covenants* book or CD-ROM (lesson 6).

- **I Can Learn More about Jesus and His Commandments as I Read the Scriptures** (2 Nephi 32:3; *Primary 1*, lesson 41; *Primary 6*, lesson 37).
- **As I Follow Jesus, My Faith Grows** (2 Nephi 31:10; *Primary 2*, lesson 15; *Primary 4*, lesson 22).

JESUS CHRIST PERFORMED MIRACLES Three Miracles Picture Poster in the *Primary Partners New Testament* book or CD-ROM (lesson 16).

I WILL BE BLESSED AS I READ THE SCRIPTURES AND KEEP THE COMMANDMENTS Sticker Challenge in the *Primary Partners Old Testament* book or CD-ROM (less. 37).

Copy the above images from the *Primary Partners Teaching Tools-I Belong to The Church of Jesus Christ of Latter-day Saints* book, or print in color or black & white from the CD-ROM. Or, copy or print the images from the corresponding *Primary Partners* books or CD-ROMs.

Theme 8   I'll Honor His Name — Mosiah 5:8

- **I Take the Name of Jesus Christ upon Me When I Am Baptized**
  (D&C 18:22; 20:37; *Primary 4*, lessons 10, 12).
- **When I Take the Sacrament, I Renew My Baptismal Covenants: I Promise to Keep the Lord's Commandments and Always Remember Him** (D&C 20:77, 79; *Primary 3*, lesson 32, 33).

I WILL BE VALIANT AND TELL OTHERS ABOUT JESUS What Would Jesus Do? Choice Situation Sack in the *Primary Partners Book of Mormon* book or CD-ROM (lesson 8).

I WILL REMEMBER JESUS Sacrament Symbols Two-sided Puzzle in the *Primary Partners Book of Mormon* book or CD-ROM (lesson 36).

I WILL THINK OF JESUS Testimony Building Blocks Puzzle in the *Primary Partners New Testament* book or CD-ROM (lesson 29).

- **I Will Use the Names of Heavenly Father and Jesus Reverently**
  (Exodus 20:7; *Primary 3*, lesson 43).

HEAVENLY FATHER HELPS ME AS I OBEY Commandment Concentration in the *Primary Partners Book of Mormon* book or CD-ROM (lesson 3).

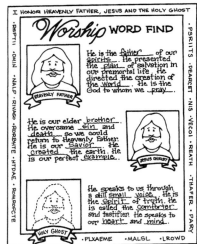

I HONOR HEAVENLY FATHER, JESUS CHRIST, AND THE HOLY GHOST Who Do I Worship? Word Find in the *Primary Partners Old Testament* book or CD-ROM (lesson 34).

Theme 9   I'll Do What is Right – Deuteronomy 6:18

- **I Can Know When the Holy Ghost Is Helping Me Choose the Right** (Moroni 10:5; *Primary 3*, lesson 26; *Primary 6*, lesson 27).
- **Choose One or Two of the Principles from** *My Gospel Standards* **to Present Each Week.**

JESUS SPEAKS TO ME THROUGH THE HOLY GHOST Find the Spirit of Truth Cross Match in the *Primary Partners Old Testament* book or CD-ROM (lesson 27).

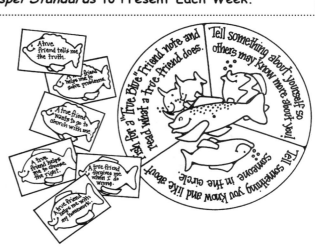

I WILL LIVE WORTHY TO RECEIVE PRIESTHOOD BLESSINGS My Gospel Standards Sentence Search in the *Primary Partners Old Testament* book or CD-ROM (less. 47).

I CAN BE A TRUE FRIEND TO JESUS AND OTHERS Fishing for a Friend Spin-and-tell in the *Primary Partners Old Testament* book or CD-ROM (lesson 29).

I WILL MAKE AND KEEP GOOD PROMISES Honesty Pays Blessings Bucks Board Game in the *Primary Partners Old Testament* book or CD-ROM (lesson 14).

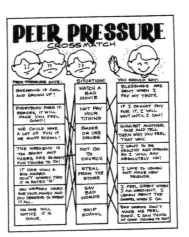

I WILL BE A POSITIVE INFLUENCE ON MY FRIENDS Peer Pressure Cross Match Puzzle in the *Primary Partners Old Testament* book or CD-ROM (lesson 32).

I WILL KEEP THIS LAW OF HEALTH Word of Wisdom Choices Match Puzzle in the *Primary Partners Old Testament* book or CD-ROM (less. 40).

Theme 10   I'll Follow His Light – John 14:6

> ● **Jesus Lights the Way as My Example** (3 Nephi 18:16).
> ● **Jesus Lights the Ways with His Teachings** (D&C 84:45-46; *Primary 7*, lessons 10, 12).

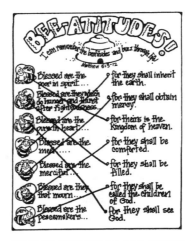

I WILL FOLLOW JESUS Footstep Flash Cards in the *Primary Partners New Testament* book or CD-ROM (lesson 23).

OTHERS TESTIFY THAT JESUS IS GOD'S SON Testimonies of Jesus Scripture Picture Match Game in the *Primary Partners New Testament* book or CD-ROM (less. 28).

JESUS TAUGHT US HOW TO RETURN TO HEAVEN "Bee"-atitude Cross Match in the *Primary Partners New Testament* book or CD-ROM (lesson 10).

THE GOSPEL OF JESUS CHRIST IS MY SURE FOUNDATION Rock and Body Puzzle in the *Primary Partners New Testament* book or CD-ROM (less. 12).

> ● **I Will Follow His Light and Be an Example** (3 Nephi 18:24; *Primary 1*, lesson 36; *Primary 2*, lesson 29).
> ● **As I Follow His Light, I Am Protected** (Psalm 27:1; *Primary 4*, lessons 25, 26).

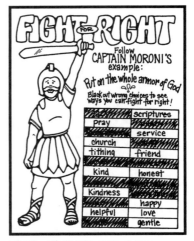

I CAN FOLLOW JESUS AND OBEY Heavenly Treasure Hunt in the *Primary Partners CTR–A* book or CD-ROM (less. 30).

THE ARMOR OF GOD WILL PROTECT ME FROM EVIL Fight for Right! Word Choice in the *Primary Partners Book of Mormon* book or CD-ROM (less. 25).

Theme 11   Teachings of the Prophet – Amos 3:7

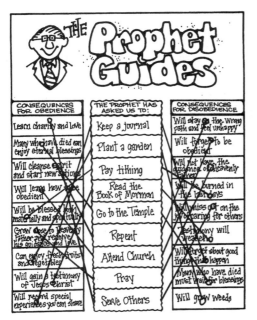

I WILL LISTEN TO THE PROPHET
The Prophet Guides Choices and
Consequences Cross Match in the
*Primary Partners Doctrine and
Covenants* book or CD-ROM (less. 31).

**I WILL TRUST IN THE LORD AND
OBEY** Follow Righteous Leaders Trust-
and-Tell Game in the *Primary Partners
Old Testament* book or CD-ROM
(lesson 24).

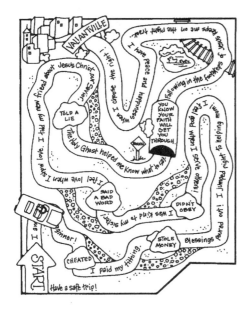

**I WILL STAY ON THE RIGHT
ROAD TO HAPPINESS** Valiant-ville
"Convert"-able Obstacle Course in the
Primary Partners New Testament book
or CD-ROM (lesson 42).

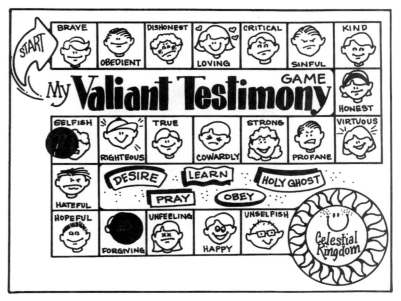

THE GOSPEL OF JESUS CHRIST IS TRUE Valiant
Testimony Board Game in the *Primary Partners Old
Testament* book or CD-ROM (lesson 41).

Copy the above images from the *Primary Partners Teaching Tools-I Belong to The Church of Jesus Christ of Latter-day Saints* book,
or print in color or black & white from the CD-ROM. Or, copy or print the images from the corresponding *Primary Partners* books or CD-ROMs.

Theme 12   His Truth I Will Proclaim

- **What Is a Testimony? I Can Have a Testimony of Jesus Christ, His Gospel, and His Church** (D&C 76:22; *Primary 4*, lessons 33, 44; *Primary 5*, lesson 46).
- **I Can Share the Gladness of the Gospel with Others** (D&C 84:62; *Primary 2*, less. 11; *Primary 4*, less. 17).

I WILL BE VALIANT AND TESTIFY OF JESUS
Valiant Testimony Balloon Maze in the *Primary Partners New Testament* book or CD-ROM (less. 43).

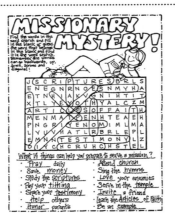

I WILL PREPARE NOW TO SHARE THE GOSPEL WITH OTHERS
Missionary Mystery! Word Search in the *Primary Partners New Testament* book or CD-ROM (lesson 44).

- **I Am Grateful for the Savior and the Blessings of My Membership in His Church** (Mosiah 2:41; *Primary 1*, lesson 42; *Primary 3*, lesson 21).

I WILL PREPARE FOR MY MISSION
Missionary Doors Scripture Search in the *Primary Partners Old Testament* book or CD-ROM (lesson 9).

HEAVENLY FATHER WANTS EVERYONE TO LEARN THE GOSPEL
My Mission Statement Message Decode in the *Primary Partners New Testament* book or CD-ROM (less. 40).

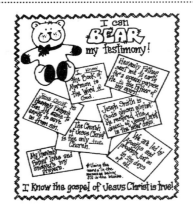

I CAN "BEAR" MY TESTIMONY
Find the Secret Message Poster in the *Primary Partners New Testament* book or CD-ROM (lesson 37).